Selected Poems of E. J. Pratt

Selected Poems of
E. J. PRATT

Edited and with an
introduction, bibliography,
and notes by
PETER BUITENHUIS

Macmillan of Canada / Toronto

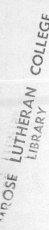

© The Macmillan Company of Canada Limited 1968

ISBN 7705-0394-2

Library of Congress Catalog Card Number 68-13877

Printed in Canada by Ronalds-Federated Ltd.
for the Macmillan Company of Canada Limited,
70 Bond Street, Toronto.

Reprinted 1969, 1972

PREFACE

The idea for this volume originated when I was helping to create a syllabus for the first Canadian Literature course to be given in the English Language and Literature Honours Course at the University of Toronto, in 1963. I wish to thank Mr. Robin Strachan, and Mr. Patrick Meany of The Macmillan Company of Canada for encouraging me to proceed with it. I would like also to thank the staff of the Victoria College Library, particularly Miss Edith Honey, for their help in compiling the bibliography, Mr. Frank Cebulski of the Graduate School at the University of California for his assistance in checking texts and notes, and Mrs. Viola Pratt and Miss Claire Pratt for the chronology of the poet's life. The text of the poems is that of the second edition of *The Collected Poems of E. J. Pratt*, edited by Northrop Frye.

CONTENTS

EDWIN JOHN PRATT – CHRONOLOGY

(For publications see pp. 207–10)

1882	Born at Western Bay, Newfoundland, February 4. Son of the Rev. John Pratt, Yorkshire-born clergyman, and Fanny Knight, daughter of a Newfoundland sea captain.
1888–1901	Educated in outport schools and at St. John's Methodist College, with a three-year intermission as a draper's apprentice (1896–1898).
1901–4	Teacher at Moreton's Harbour, a whaling village in Notre Dame Bay.
1904–7	Preacher–probationer in the Methodist ministry, at Clarke's Beach, Bell Island, and Portugal Cove.
1907–11	Student in Philosophy, Victoria College, University of Toronto.
1912	Received M.A. degree. Thesis: Demonology.
1913	Received B.D. degree. Ordained into the Methodist ministry.
1913–20	Demonstrator in Psychology at University of Toronto. Assistant Minister in number of churches around Streetsville, Ontario.
1917	Received Ph.D. degree from University of Toronto. Thesis: Studies in Pauline eschatology.
1918	Married Viola Whitney.
1920	Joined Department of English, Victoria College.
1921	Birth of only child, Mildred Claire.
1930	Elected to Royal Society of Canada. Taught in summer schools of Dalhousie,

	Queen's University, and the University of British Columbia, 1930–52.
1936	One of the founders and first editor (until 1942) of *Canadian Poetry* magazine.
1937	Won the Governor General's Annual Literary Award for *The Fable of the Goats*.
1940	Awarded the Lorne Pierce Medal for distinguished services to Canadian literature and a second Governor General's Award.
1946	In the King's Honours List, created Commander of the Order of St. Michael and St. George.
1952	Received the Governor General's Award for *Towards the Last Spike*, and from the University of Alberta, a gold medal for distinguished service to Canadian literature.
1953	Retired from Victoria College. Received Honorary LL.D. from University of Toronto.
1961	Received the Canada Council Medal for distinction in the field of literature.
1964	Died in Toronto, April 26.

INTRODUCTION

As Northrop Frye said in his lucid introduction to the second edition of the *Collected Poems*, E. J. Pratt cannot be sampled in anthologies. It is in the hope of making his work more readily available to students and the general reader that I have made this comprehensive selection from his lyrical and long poems and added also some critical apparatus. It may be that the most significant part of this volume will be the selected bibliography, particularly of the work so far done on Pratt. Most, if not all, of the serious critical writing on Pratt's poetry has been included, and a quick check by the reader will reveal how little there is of it. Pratt did not lack fame in his native land during his lifetime, but he did lack then, and has done since, informed analysis and commentary.

A contributory factor to this situation has been Ned Pratt's renownedly social personality, his gift for the anecdote, and his personal charm. As a beginning professor of English at Victoria College, I was at once made aware of this; for, although he had retired from teaching at the College some years before, Ned kept up the habit of lunching there twice a week so long as he could make it down to the Senior Common Room. His gift for friendship, even for someone so much younger than himself, was astonishing and I, along with the other lunchers at that good table, basked in the warmth of his benevolence and the glow of his stories. And yet, I was later to recall that short story of Henry James, "The Private Life", which he based on his observation of Robert Browning. James observed the diner-out Browning, smooth, debonair, eminently social, then turned to the poetry to find the image of a complex, difficult, even lonely individual. He could only reconcile the two Brownings by inventing an *alter ego*, a serious shade who sat upstairs at the writing-table while the social mask went down to dinner. Something of this "doppelgänger" quality was, I think, in Pratt's personality. Most of the studies that I have found stress his sociability, and they repeat, sometimes *ad nauseam*, the anecdotes that attached themselves like limpets to the poet, particularly to his Newfoundland days. The *alter ego* has consequently suffered in isolation as the commentators have caroused with the smiling public man downstairs.

Earle Birney has acutely and entertainingly analysed the vicissitudes of Pratt's reputation in "E. J. Pratt and His Critics", so I do not have to rehearse the strange tale of the alternate ignorings and misreadings that have plagued the poet's works.* Pratt's simplicity, like that of Blake, to whom one critic has compared him, is sometimes deceptive. On the other hand, to dwell on the complex layers of religious symbolic interpretation, as John Sutherland does in his book, is to slight Pratt's primary concern with narrative. There are subtleties of meaning within the poems that call for considerable explication, but Pratt's work does not yield much to the strategies of critics searching for ambiguities. The Winter 1964 number of *Canadian Literature* indicates that close study of his work is at last properly under way, but even these articles are sometimes marred by attempts to "place" Pratt neatly within a religious or myth-making pigeon-hole.

In order fully to enter and appreciate the poetic world of Edwin John Pratt, it is necessary first to take his intellectual bearings which, for most modern readers, have already begun to get confused. Fred Cogswell has

*Full citations for the books and articles referred to in this introduction can be found in the bibliography on pages 207–10 of this volume.

called Pratt "the last-born literary child of frontier America", and there is a good deal of truth in that jocular observation. He belongs in a tradition that is far more American than British, and far more western than eastern, for all his Atlantic-seaboard birth. In his philosophical outlook, at least, Pratt is close to the Californian writers Jack London, Frank Norris, and Robinson Jeffers, particularly the two novelists. They tended to see human relations in terms of force, nature in terms of tooth and claw, and history in terms of growth. Their authority for this view came originally from Darwin's *The Origin of Species* (1859), but more directly from Herbert Spencer's popularization and, in some respects, falsification of Darwin's work in such books as *The Factors of Organic Evolution* (1887) and *The Principles of Sociology* (1891). Coining the key phrase "the survival of the fittest", Spencer translated Darwin's geological and biological concepts into human terms and placed his faith in the evolutionary principle working in human society – a kind of impersonal force that seems to have the sanction of some remote, divine origin.

Given the formative stage of society in North America, it is not surprising that Spencer's works were far more influential here than in his native England. His ideas permeated the consciousness of well-educated people in the United States at the end of the nineteenth century and, allowing for cultural lag, spread to Canada early in the twentieth century. In the still primitive conditions of the Far West and the Canadian eastern seaboard, the wilderness of plain, desert, sea, and rock gave a meaningful setting to the clash of forces taking place within society too. Pratt's work is filled with images of primitive nature and evolutionary history. It seemed instinctive to him to write of molluscs, of cetacean and cephalod, of Java and Piltdown Man. The evolutionary process early became and always remained the central metaphor of Pratt's work. It gave him the themes for his best lyrics and provided him with the solid framework within which he could achieve an epic style. The evolutionary metaphor persisted in Pratt's work long after it had ceased to have much force for the twentieth-century poetic and philosophic mind.

The reasons for this are not difficult to find. Pratt, the son of a Methodist minister, was headed for the church, and wrote his doctoral thesis at the University of Toronto on the eschatology of St. Paul – that is to say, the Saint's doctrine of "last things": death, judgement, heaven, and hell. Although Pratt was actually ordained, at some point in his career he, like a number of nineteenth-century English poets, underwent a crisis of belief. Although the Old and New Testaments remained to supply important ideals and images in his work, they did not remain convincing enough to make him the Christian humanist that both Northrop Frye and John Sutherland have claimed him to be. On the other hand, Vincent Sharman's contention that Pratt thought the deity of God and the divinity of Christ to be merely illusory seems to throw the baby out with the bath-water. Pratt could not completely reject his early upbringing and training, and he did maintain a kind of wonder in the presence of nature and man's potential that amounts at least to a reverent agnosticism. The two poems singled out by Sharman to substantiate Pratt's atheism, *The Iron Door* and *Brébeuf and His Brethren,* can be read in an entirely different way. Sharman says that "the door [to the afterlife] opens because those who create it can do with it as they wish: the door is the petitioners' own illusion, and their further illusion will see it opened." If this is so, the illusion is given a remarkably creative power. Pratt writes:

> And while it was not given me to know
> Whither their journey led, I had caught the sense
> Of life with high auroras and the flow
> Of wide majestic spaces;
> Of light abundant; and of keen impassioned faces,
> Transfigured underneath its vivid glow.

Sharman quotes the last three lines of the poem as evidence that Pratt "cannot participate in the revelation

of the Afterlife", but the context of those last three lines —
the unquoted four that precede it — are equally important.
The door closes behind the dead:

> But neither gird of hinges, nor the feel of air
> Returning with its drizzled weight of cloud,
> Could cancel half the meaning of that hour, —
> Not though the vision passed away,
> And I was left alone, aware
> Of blindness falling with terrestrial day
> On sight enfeebled by the solar glare.

Pratt does not commit himself either to a denial or to an
affirmation of the afterlife, but he does show that belief
itself is a reality that can transform life and give even
the sceptical earth-bound mind a vision of beauty and
meaning.

Similarly, Sharman's claim that Brébeuf's source of
strength is "in the self-glorification signified by the sound
of the trumpets" in his vision of the crucifixion at his
martyrdom does not bear examination. Descendant of
warriors that he is, Brébeuf (like T. S. Eliot's Becket)
has to fight as hard against pride in his own power as he
does against the savagery and paganism of the Indians.
His martyrdom signifies the conquest of self and is not so
much fulfilment of what Sharman calls "his conscious
wish to die" as acceptance of the consequences of his
overwhelming need to convert the savages. Sharman
reads the conclusion to *Brébeuf*, "The Martyrs' Shrine",
as a bitter indictment of twentieth-century Canadians.
Even though the Jesuits may have been misguided, he
writes, "they had the strength of determination to accept
a great challenge". Those who have built the shrine "are
pallid beside those they honour". This is a curious interpretation of an epilogue that celebrates the years that
"have ripened the martyrs' seed", and commemorates the
trails sunk under "the mould of the centuries" which
later blossom "into the highways that lead to the crest of
the hill". If a poet's imagery means anything at all, it is
surely to be interpreted in a way that makes sense of these

symbols of growth and achievement. The significance of *Brébeuf and His Brethren* for contemporary Canadians is precisely that the hardships and horrors of the three-hundred-year-old mission did not end in the apparent failure of the burning of Sainte Marie, but provided the example and the tradition on which a nation could build. The implicit analogy is the legend of the phoenix. When, at the shrine, "the Aves / And prayers ascend, and the Holy Bread is broken", we are surely not listening, as Sharman would have it, to "a last, almost wearied comment on the illusion of those responsible for the shrine and on the illusion which the shrine perpetuates", but to the affirmation of the continuity of history and the transforming power of belief.

Pratt's belief in evolutionary theory, as well as his studies in psychology and anthropology, led him towards relativism and agnosticism; at the same time, his upbringing and his own studies in Pauline eschatology influenced him to look for final causes. His was a characteristic response of those who had gone through a crisis of belief. Loren Eiseley has shown, in *Darwin's Century* (1958), that time and again philosophers and scientists have substituted some other metaphysical explanation for the universe after evolutionary theory had broken down the authority of the Bible for them. In his article on Pratt, Paul West has written: "To read his epics attentively, trying to respond to all those whales, icebergs, dinosaurs, giants and storms, is to attempt one's own studies in Prattian eschatology." The clearest example of this is "The Truant" in which puny man appears as a creature endowed with gigantic resistance. The ALL HIGH of the poem, Professor Frye has pointed out, thinks himself God, but is only the mechanical power of the universe. This somewhat comic deity, who speaks in evolutionary terms and metaphors, has man hauled before him to be punished for messing up the grand evolving scheme of things. Cheeky *genus homo*, instead of being duly cowed by the great Panjandrum, points out that He is largely man's invention in any case. While not denying the mechanistic force that the Panjandrum represents, man, in a defiant last speech, refuses to join the Lord's ballet and dares Him to do his worst.

The poem is too simplistic to be convincing, but it is essential reading for anyone who seeks to understand Pratt's thought. His unerring sense of the physical scale of things, from iceberg down to wren, accurately placed puny, mortal man where he belonged. On the other hand, Pratt believed that man's intelligence and his will to endure, developed through centuries of torture, warfare, and natural disasters, made him sufficient to conquer any obstacle that a Panjandrum or anything else can put in his way. Pratt celebrates vigorously many things in the universe, from the flight of the eagle down to the deepest sounding of the whale, but his best praise is reserved for man – man beset, exhausted, killed, but ultimately victorious.

A poet's religious views do not determine the quality of his work, nor do they have much to do with his enduring reputation. As W. H. Auden pointed out, in his elegy on W. B. Yeats, time

> Worships language and forgives
> Everyone by whom it lives . . .
> Time that with this strange excuse
> Pardoned Kipling and his views,
> And will pardon Paul Claudel
> Pardons him for writing well.

Pratt's ethical viewpoint, although dated even during his own lifetime, will not necessarily date him in future years. Fred Cogswell, in attempting to predict the course of Pratt's reputation, has called his poetic vision "almost incredibly primitive" and has compared him to Bliss Carman, whose fame plummeted so disastrously after his death. This kind of prognostication is about as dependable as plunging in speculative stocks. However, it is fruitful to attempt to isolate those qualities that give Pratt claim to an enduring reputation. Cogswell himself has stated that "technical pre-eminence is all the greatness that can be assigned" to him but, depending on how we define technique, that can be a very great deal. Cogswell does little more than state that Pratt used "a language of scientific description" and "a grammatical syntax and a metrical rhythm" that were suited to his age; but analyses of the poems readily reveal that Pratt is doing that and usually a good deal more.

To read *Brébeuf* closely is soon to become aware of the strength of its design. How skilfully, for example, Pratt moves from seventeenth-century France, drawn for us with a few deft touches, to the western hemisphere, again sketched in with almost magical felicity in phrases like:

> at the equinoxes
> Under the gold and green of the auroras
> Wild geese drove wedges through the zodiac.

The poem is put together in a mosaic form usually under yearly dates, which chart the triumphs and the heart-breaks of the missionaries. It is carefully built piece by piece so that an overwhelming sense of the myriad problems faced by the Jesuits is conveyed. From the 1635 section on, the tension slowly mounts as the reader is made more and more aware of the terrible and inevitable destruction that will come upon the priests. The succession of captures, torturings, and murders works towards its climax in the martyrdom of Brébeuf. The priests scarcely emerge as individuals, as is fitting. Theirs is a joint venture, and the successes and sufferings are shared alike. At the same time they become representatives of historical forces, symbols of stages of civilization, as do the Indians, so that the conflict between them is both elemental and unavoidable. Yet the poem is saved from impersonality by the innumerable touches of specific detail, ceremonials, meals, vegetation, lodge-construction, language, and gesture. It is moved forward by a tremendous narrative energy that Pratt, almost alone among twentieth-century poets, possesses. The blank verse is fairly heavily allitera-tive, but not oppressively so. The rhythms are beautifully varied by many run-on lines, and their harmony is established with a sure control of assonance and contrast. Close analysis will also reveal the skill with which Pratt adapts the rich variety of syntactical patterns inherent in English to the demands of his metrics.

Above all, one is aware in reading *Brébeuf* of the innumerable gems of phrase, such as (a random sampling) "the subtle savagery of art", "the rosary against the amulet", "hermit thrushes rivalled the rapture of the nightingales", "gardens and pastures rolling like a sea / From Lisieux to Le Havre". Notice how, in each of these phrases, the broad themes and conflicts of the poem are suggested, how in the least metaphor or image reverberations are started that sound throughout the poem and establish its rich texture and closely-knit form.

Through his mastery of technique, Pratt welds form to theme. In its largest concern *Brébeuf* is about French imperialism in North America. The duality of its theme is mirrored in the warrior-priest, Brébeuf himself. The references to Richelieu, Mazarin, and the lilies of France demonstrate Pratt's ever-present concern with the secular as well as the sacred and serve ironically to show that, to some extent at least, the Jesuits were being used by the French ministers of the Crown to further their dreams of empire. A converted native population would be a friendly one, and the importance of Indian alliances in the struggle between the French, Dutch, and British for control of North America can hardly be overstated. In the French and Indian Wars of the eighteenth century the combination of French soldiers and Iroquois warriors was to bring France as close to winning the continent as she ever was before Wolfe finally put an end to those ambitions with his capture of Quebec in 1759.

The theme of the poem is given a further ironic dimension in Pratt's insistence on the gap between the French and Indians along the scale of evolution. The Frenchmen are the products of centuries of culture and learning. Behind Brébeuf and his brethren stands the enormous achievement of the French medieval cathedral-builders, artists, and theologians, the traditions of chivalric warfare, and the splendours of Renaissance cuisine and viniculture. The disparity between this complex culture and the filthy primitivism of the Indians (best shown by Brébeuf's letter to France) not only stresses the enormous difficulty of the Jesuits' task, but also underlines the virtual certainty of its failure.

Pratt's narrative demonstrates how closely a tribe's or a nation's religion is a product of its culture and needs, and establishes a real sympathy for the bewildered natives. Obviously a religion that promises a heaven without hunting, war, feasts, and tobacco was about as useful to the Indian as a tomahawk without a blade. Only the Jesuits' resort to the primitive symbolism of the Christian Hell could make much impression on his imagination. Again and again the Jesuits are forced to oversimplify and substitute to get even the crudest notions of their religion across. What happens, in effect, is that they have to go backwards many years along the path of evolution to make any contact with the savages. The ultimate meeting of minds of Jesuit and Indian comes not in terms of belief but on the common ground of physical endurance. One after another the priests go to their excruciating deaths, torn and racked by tortures that surpass in refinement even those of the Medici. (In this field, at least, the Indians have an edge over Renaissance man.) No wonder that the most effective parts of the poem deal with details of torture. Pratt stresses that it was no mean achievement of Christian belief and culture to arm men more effectively against refined torments than the most stoic endurance of the Iroquois warrior code could ever do. The final magnificent set-piece of Brébeuf's torture – which Goya has also commemorated in a horrifying painting – shows how the priest reverts to his warrior heritage, becomes a lion at bay and gives his foes "roar for roar" until he conquers this secular source of defiance to come to rely at the last on the vision of that earlier crucifixion.

The Indians were finally subdued not, of course, by Christianity, but by those other gifts of civilization:

smallpox, pox, whisky, and firearms. But, for Pratt, the heroism of the Jesuits survived their extermination and becomes epic material as well as the legend out of which a nation constructs its ideal past. One of the major implications of the poem is that the French contribution to the Canadian (even the Ontario) past is imperishably important and enduringly significant.

Brébeuf and His Brethren is in most ways the peak of E. J. Pratt's art, but one can see in other long poems the way in which he marries his technique to his themes. Notice how in *The Titanic* the gambling motif is echoed again and again: in the captain's gamble for the blue riband, his gamble on the effectiveness of the new device, the radio, in the engineers' gamble with the supposedly foolproof hydraulic rams in closing the watertight doors. These gambles are given an ironic dimension by the superbly dramatized poker game among the passengers. In each case the unexpected happens, and man's presumption is met by defeat, just as the Titans' attempt to dethrone the Olympian gods had met with ruin. Again the poem is organized through contrasts, primarily that of the apparently secure, warm, luxurious world of the liner against the menacing, icy, primal world of sea and berg. Within that there is the contrast between the intricate, technical, and professional aspect of the liner's mechanism and the elaborate richness of its accommodations and food. In his short poem on the same subject, "The Convergence of the Twain", Thomas Hardy typically concentrates on the fatal aspect of the disaster, ship and iceberg being the "twin halves of one august event". Pratt, while including the apparently fatal signs in the building and launching of the ship, concentrates subsequently on the power of chance, even though in his own note to the poem (see pp. 213–14) he talks of the "web of Fate" that tightened round the ship. Chance allied with *hubris* brings about the collision, and once more serves to remind his readers that, however far man may be along the evolutionary road, he cannot escape the fact and power of nature.

In *Towards the Last Spike*, which I have included here in a shortened version, the lesson is the same. In this poem man has the chance to learn from his mistakes and to employ his sinews and his technology gradually to throw his thin lines of steel across muskeg and mountain. Again Pratt is using a mosaic technique of organizing his diverse material; but because *Towards the Last Spike* contains a good deal of political material, it is looser in form than the other epics. The gigantic nature of his theme tends to make the poem too impersonal, even though forces like the North Shore Laurentian monster and Lady British Columbia are personified, just as Frank Norris personified the wheat and the railroad in *The Octopus*. Fortunately, the gigantism of these forces is almost matched by the human figures that Pratt has chosen as his heroes, William Van Horne and Sir John A. Macdonald. The two men are complementary in the poem: Macdonald, rhetorician and parliamentarian, supplies the dream of continental union; Van Horne, engineer and administrator, supplies the force and skill that make the dream come true. In editing the poem I have cut substantially from the political part and left the engineering part almost intact, for Pratt characteristically seemed more at home with the making than with the talking. If this slights the role of the Canadian and favours the American, I have to beg pardon of the historians with the excuse that, in the epic tradition, Nestor has always had to make way for Achilles.

Pratt's taste for action on a Homeric scale is fully realized in the animal epic, *The Cachalot*. The whale of a hero is even, in the Homeric manner, given a pedigree that fully establishes his title to nobility and heroism:

> The great grandsire – a veteran rover –
> Had entered once the strait of Dover,
> In a naval fight, and with his hump
> Had stove a bottom of Van Tromp;

Here, as elsewhere in the poem, Pratt exploits the comic incongruities of rhyme and off-rhyme and the slightly galloping effect of pounding iambic and alliterative tetrameter. Also in *The Cachalot* Pratt is at his best in the comic juxtaposition of disparate material, for example, nautical and anatomical in

>   and so large
> The lymph-flow of his active liver,
> One might believe a fair-sized barge
> Could navigate along the river

and mythological and geographical in

> Where the Acherontic flood
> Of sepia, mingling with the blood
> Of whale, befouled Delgado's sides.

It is startling to discover that, according to E. K. Brown, Pratt had not read Herman Melville's *Moby Dick* when he wrote *The Cachalot*, for the excitement and rhetorical richness of the poem seem amazingly similar to the prose epic. In particular, Pratt's picture of the whale swimming towards the equator accompanied by seagulls, at the end of Part II, is extraordinarily like the appearance of the white whale in Chapter CXXXIII of *Moby Dick*. Similarities of temperament (even Pratt's gusto seems more appropriate to the nineteenth than the twentieth century), their common love of the sea, and their fascination with the forces of the universe led both men to seek out the most appropriate symbol for their vision. Nature's largest creature was their logical choice. The major difference between the narratives of *Moby Dick* and *The Cachalot* – aside from their length – is that Melville's whale survives the encounter with the whale ship. Moby Dick is in fact so much more than mere natural force that Melville invests him with the profoundest mysteries of being.

Melville's conception of heroism is also quite different from Pratt's. The members of the crew of the *Pequod* are so caught up in the mighty personality of Ahab that their individualities are swept into his. Even the *isolato*, Ishmael, becomes one with the common body devoted to the destruction of the whale. Ahab's quenchless feud and unutterable woe give him a tragic dimension that can be found nowhere in Pratt's work. A tragic writer must be saturated with a concern for the fate of the individual. For all his treatment of heroic action, Pratt could never interest himself sufficiently in the tragic nature of the individual case.

The war poem, *Behind the Log*, shows this clearly. As in *Brébeuf* there is no distinct hero. Heroic virtue has so far been diffused amongst the crews of merchantman and warship that Pratt talks of men

> with surnames blotted by their jobs
> Into a scrawl of anonymity . . .
> Who had become incorporate with the cogs
> On ships that carried pulp and scrap to Europe.

Pratt's subject in *Behind the Log* is highly congenial to his philosophical point of view. It is the passage of a great convoy of freighters and escorts through the U-boat-infested waters of the North Atlantic. As the Commodore says:

> *While it is true that for the navigation*
> *Of his own ship each master must be held*
> *Responsible, there is but little room*
> *For rugged individualists.*

The safety of all depends on absolute obedience and good drill, although even these are largely powerless against the wolf-pack techniques of the submarines. Once again, Pratt has found his theme in a conflict of forces that is expressed in almost primitive terms. The German sailors are just as determined and disciplined as the Allies, and what finally counts in the struggle is the strongest force. At the end the five British destroyers race up and tip the balance. The victory of force does not negate the individual acts of heroism, but Pratt again and again stresses that in such huge movements of men and materials, the record can scarcely pause long enough to include the individual act. What go into the log-book are the multitudinous nautical facts:

> The temperature of the sea forty degrees,
> The lowering falls are clear, boats off the pins ...

Behind the log are the innumerable human facts that will never reach the records, the headlines, or the pages of history, but make up in their immense and staggering total the effort that finally wins the war against Nazi tyranny. The best way that Pratt knows of chronicling this process is by the infinitely faithful reporting of naval ways, techniques, and language and by the awful glimpses of human agony as men are drowned, burned in oil, and entombed in steel. *Behind the Log* stands, with Nicholas Monsarrat's *The Cruel Sea*, as the outstanding account of convoy duty in the Second World War.

Pratt's lyrics do not in general command the same interest with his readers as his long poems, in which he could more easily get into his splendid stride. But some of his lyrics are fine achievements of precision and perception. It is a truism of Pratt criticism that the most fruitful fount of lyric poetry – love – seemed dry to him. As Henry James said of Emerson, after a trip through the Louvre during which the philosopher seemed singularly unappreciative of the paintings: "there were certain chords in Emerson that did not vibrate at all". Poetically, at least, the chord of love was singularly silent in Pratt. In fact, almost the only poem about love in the *Collected Poems* is "Like Mother, Like Daughter". The ambivalence of Pratt's feeling about the ruling passion is expressed in the third stanza:

> You caught the *male* for good or ill,
> And locked him in a golden cage ...

and the last:

> But whether joy or whether woe –
> Lure of lips or scorn of eyes –
> We bless you either way we go,
> In or out of Paradise.

Readers will also note the reference to Keats's forlorn

knight-at-arms in the first stanza and the catastrophic overtones of his list of women at the beginning: "Helen, Deirdre, Héloïse, / Laura, Cleopatra, Eve!" For Pratt the world of women seems to represent temptation and imprisonment, while the world of men represents adventure, liberation, and the possibility of heroic action. This is made clear in the poem "Deeds" in which Pratt wonders what has happened to the beauty that inspired lovers to sing serenades, the minstrels to praise the cavalcades, and the poets to write of fruit, flowers, and birds. His own answer is that beauty for him is not in these things but in the act of heroism – the almost hopeless dive for the boy's body by an unnamed swimmer. On the whole, however, the heroic is found more often in the longer poems, where it traditionally belongs.

The lyrics frequently express Pratt's sense of man's ironic fate in a mechanized world, as in "The Man and the Machine". He may be in control of a locomotive, streamlined and "with cougar-grace", but his pulses are "lesioned" with the effort to control the machine, and his face is mired with slag. Pratt seems to be implying that the machine age has demoted some of its servants to the stone age again. The shadow line between cave-man and civilized man is best expressed in Pratt's most successful lyric, "From Stone to Steel", a marvellously compact poem about man's endless journey along the evolutionary road, which may be, Pratt hints, a circle instead of a straight line.

The journey of man leads also to death, of which Pratt frequently shows a grave, even oppressive, awareness in the short poems. This is mitigated by irony in a poem like "The Drag-Irons", in which the dead captain comes up from Davy Jones's locker "with livid silence and with glassy look" – a parody of his long years of command. A poem on the same subject of a very different tone is "Come Not the Seasons Here", one of Pratt's quietest and most subtly effective works. Perhaps the poem gets its initial impulse from Shakespeare's song "Come Away Death" (which provides the title for another of his poems), but the imagery does not concern itself with death directly, but with the seasons. However, the traditional sense of growth associated with spring, summer, and autumn is undercut by the images that he chooses: cuckoo, poppy, shed bloom, sere leaf, brown pastures. Finally the kingdom of death imperiously takes over in the winter of the last stanza, in frozen air and glacial stone. The cadences of this poem are among the most haunting of any I have read, and demonstrate Pratt's mastery of his craft.

His saturation in the evolutionary theory seems to be largely responsible for his animal poems. "Silences" is a glimpse into the utter ferocity of the marine world, where "the ultimate economy of rage" expresses itself not in the sound of conflict but in the noiselessness of the kill. How different this is from that later development of the evolutionary cycle, the land mammals, in whom warm blood produces snarls and, ultimately, hearty oaths. Yet Pratt suggests in the last part of this chilling poem that there lies a layer of silence in every creature that harks back to the earliest stages of primeval ferocity. This is portrayed in the silent, deadly circling of dog and cat. "Silences" is one of Pratt's rare excursions into the realm of free-verse, a looseness of form that is appropriate to the reflective structure of the thought and the primitive form of its emotions.

Pratt's other animals are given the discipline of rhyme. "The Prize Cat" is the animal version of "From Stone to Steel", and its whimsical beginning effectively underlines the terror of the last stanza. On the other hand, Carlo, the Newfoundland dog, seems to be arguing by his actions that he is moving higher in the evolutionary scale, not harking back, like the cat, to savage origins. The dying eagle seems to be a parable about the ever-extending domain of man through the evolving powers of his technology. The eagle, king till now of the domain of mountains, sees in the flight of the plane his kingdom lost. Though the point could have been made more effectively without giving the bird a human sort of reasoning power, the poem still remains a vivid and pathetic statement, and a comment on man's complacent pride in his achievements.

It is clear that Pratt's subject matter was limited by several preoccupations and by the somewhat rigid intellectual framework within which he worked. Some historical events and literary fashions that many of his contemporaries found almost overwhelming appear to have left him untouched, poetically speaking. He was over thirty when the First World War broke out, and yet that cataclysmic event, which both made and killed many poets, seems to have left hardly a mark on his poetry. The roaring twenties, which in turn brought forth its crop of responsive recorders, seems not to have had any effect on his work. The following economic depression of the thirties seems to have had only one response, "The Depression Ends". Here, instead of inveighing against the economic and social dislocation that had caused such misery, Pratt realizes "a mad chimera" and changes "a world predestinate" to poverty into a Homeric feast that brings to each not only unlimited food and drink but also a stomach that does not "turn traitor on its appetite".

Stranger still is the absence from Pratt's works of a marked response to the rapidly changing forms of literary taste. Stylistically Pratt remained a contemporary of Tennyson and Thomas Hardy – except for his avoidance of archaic words and his use of technical terms of modern science and technology. The revolt in poetic diction signalled by the publication of Gerard Manley Hopkins's work in 1918 left no imprint on Pratt's work. The even greater impact of Eliot, Pound, and the later poems of Yeats made no difference to the long poems and can only be said to have had some slight effect on the diction, tone, and imagery of some of the lyrics. The social attitudes and style of the nineteen-thirties poets – not only the Englishmen Auden and Spender, but also his fellow-Canadians such as Frank Scott and A. M. Klein – have no echo in Pratt's work.

Several reasons may be advanced for this curious poetic isolation. The first is that Canada remained longer than most western nations in the backwater of modern history and literary culture. This is important for Pratt's development, perhaps, only in that in such an intellectual climate he realized his poetic vocation late in life. He was brought into the teaching of literature by Pelham Edgar after some years of teaching psychology, and was forty before his first book of poems was published. Therefore he missed much of that heady excitement that the young poet feels when he is undergoing successive waves of influence both from his forebears and his contemporaries. Certainly, in Toronto at that time (the 1920s) there was little of the sense of a buzzing literary coterie that a contemporary young writer of Pratt's talent would have found in London, Paris, or New York.

In certain respects, however, Pratt was the gainer from this literary isolation. At a time when the anti-heroic was succeeding the un-heroic theme in literature, Pratt was able to forge and maintain a vision of collective heroism that sustained him through his long poems. Although irony, ambiguity, and obscurity became the hallmark of style for many poets, Pratt was able to retain in his poetry his sense of the directness and simplicity of felt life. When psycho-analysis prompted a turning in to the mazes of the subconscious mind, Pratt went happily on in the clear daylight of the conscious. His late development also allowed him to exploit themes that seemed closed to many of his contemporaries. Twentieth-century poets have tended to be either a-historical or to have used history as a kind of rubbish dump from which they have plucked the bits and pieces that suited their imaginations. Pratt's intellectual framework enabled him to regard history as a great unfolding process from which he could select at will stories and incidents which could serve his large poetic purposes – rather in the manner of Shakespeare. He could as a result write the epics of Canadian experience, *Brébeuf* and *Towards the Last Spike*, that no other contemporary poet could possibly have tackled. Other writers seem to have felt that there was nothing much worth saying about the Canadian past: Earle Birney, for example,

> We French, we English, never lost our civil war,
> endure it still, a bloodless civil bore;
> no wounded lying about, no Whitman wanted.
> It's only by our lack of ghosts we're haunted.

Pratt has felt no lack of ghosts, and good healthy ones at that. Consequently he was able to create a usable past for the contemporary Canadian imagination. In his late years, this historical consciousness also enabled him to record, with rising indignation, the spreading cancer of Nazi tyranny and then to commemorate vigorously, in *Dunkirk* and *Behind the Log*, successive stages of its defeat.

Pratt's roots in older poetic traditions also enabled him to write descriptively and lyrically about the Canadian landscape. In this department he was, of course, preceded by poets like Bliss Carman and Archibald Lampman, but Pratt's scientific bent brought a precision to his depiction of the Canadian scene, particularly in its starkness, severity, and grandeur, that previously only painters of the Group of Seven had adequately captured. Although Pratt remained pre-eminently a poet of the sea, in particular of the rock-bound, storm-lashed Newfoundland coast that provided him with his earliest, most deeply-felt images, he emerged from this regional concern to discover the inland plains and mountains and to record them with love and fidelity. Canada did not find an adequate myth- and image-maker in poetry until E. J. Pratt arrived. It was fortunate that the peculiar and slightly anachronistic form of his imagination enabled him to fulfil this role so late in the national day, in an age when myth-makers had all but disappeared.

PETER BUITENHUIS
McGill University, Montreal.
September, 1967

Poems Chiefly Lyrical

NEWFOUNDLAND

Here the tides flow,
And here they ebb;
Not with that dull, unsinewed tread of waters
Held under bonds to move
Around unpeopled shores –
Moon-driven through a timeless circuit
Of invasion and retreat;
But with a lusty stroke of life
Pounding at stubborn gates,
That they might run
Within the sluices of men's hearts,
Leap under throb of pulse and nerve,
And teach the sea's strong voice
To learn the harmonies of new floods,
The peal of cataract,
And the soft wash of currents
Against resilient banks,
Or the broken rhythms from old chords
Along dark passages
That once were pathways of authentic fires.

Red is the sea-kelp on the beach,
Red as the heart's blood,
Nor is there power in tide or sun
To bleach its stain.
It lies there piled thick
Above the gulch-line.
It is rooted in the joints of rocks,
It is tangled around a spar,
It covers a broken rudder,
It is red as the heart's blood,
And salt as tears.

Here the winds blow,
And here they die,

3

Not with that wild, exotic rage
That vainly sweeps untrodden shores,
But with familiar breath
Holding a partnership with life,
Resonant with the hopes of spring,
Pungent with the airs of harvest.

They call with the silver fifes of the sea,
They breathe with the lungs of men,
They are one with the tides of the sea,
They are one with the tides of the heart,
They blow with the rising octaves of dawn,
They die with the largo of dusk,
Their hands are full to the overflow,
In their right is the bread of life,
In their left are the waters of death.

Scattered on boom
And rudder and weed
Are tangles of shells;
Some with backs of crusted bronze,
And faces of porcelain blue,
Some crushed by the beach stones
To chips of jade;
And some are spiral-cleft
Spreading their tracery on the sand
In the rich veining of an agate's heart;
And others remain unscarred,
To babble of the passing of the winds.

Here the crags
Meet with winds and tides —
Not with that blind interchange
Of blow for blow
That spills the thunder of insentient seas;
But with the mind that reads assault
In crouch and leap and the quick stealth,
Stiffening the muscles of the waves.
Here they flank the harbours,
Keeping watch

On thresholds, altars and the fires of home,
Or, like mastiffs,
Over-zealous,
Guard too well.

Tide and wind and crag,
Sea-weed and sea-shell
And broken rudder –
And the story is told
Of human veins and pulses,
Of eternal pathways of fire,
Of dreams that survive the night,
Of doors held ajar in storms.

THE SHARK

He seemed to know the harbour,
So leisurely he swam;
His fin,
Like a piece of sheet-iron,
Three-cornered,
And with knife-edge,
Stirred not a bubble
As it moved
With its base-line on the water.

His body was tubular
And tapered
And smoke-blue,
And as he passed the wharf
He turned,
And snapped at a flat-fish
That was dead and floating.
And I saw the flash of a white throat,
And a double row of white teeth,
And eyes of metallic grey,
Hard and narrow and slit.

Then out of the harbour,
With that three-cornered fin

5

Shearing without a bubble the water
Lithely,
Leisurely,
He swam —
That strange fish,
Tubular, tapered, smoke-blue,
Part vulture, part wolf,
Part neither — for his blood was cold.

CARLO

*"The dog that saved the lives of more than ninety persons
in that recent wreck, by swimming with a line from the
sinking vessel to the shore, well understood the importance as well as the risk of his mission." — Extract from a
Newfoundland paper.*

I see no use in not confessing —
To trace your breed would keep me guessing;
It would indeed an expert puzzle
To match such legs with a jet-black muzzle.
To make a mongrel, as you know,
It takes some fifty types or so,
And nothing in your height or length,
In stand or colour, speed or strength,
Could make me see how any strain
Could come from mastiff, bull, or Dane.
But, were I given to speculating
On pedigrees in canine rating,
I'd wager this — not from your size,
Not merely from your human eyes,
But from the way you held that cable
Within those gleaming jaws of sable,
Leaped from the taffrail of the wreck
With ninety souls upon its deck,
And with your cunning dog-stroke tore
Your path unerring to the shore —
Yes, stake my life, the way you swam,
That somewhere in your line a dam,

6

Shaped to this hour by God's own hand,
Had mated with a Newfoundland.

They tell me, Carlo, that your kind
Has neither conscience, soul, nor mind;
That reason is a thing unknown
To such as dogs; to man alone
The spark divine – he may aspire
To climb to heaven or even higher;
But God has tied around the dog
The symbol of his fate, the clog.
Thus, I have heard some preachers say –
Wise men and good, in a sort o' way –
Proclaiming from the sacred box
(Quoting from Butler and John Knox)
How freedom and the moral law
God gave to man, because He saw
A way to draw a line at root
Between the human and the brute.
And you were classed with things like bats,
Parrots and sand-flies and dock-rats,
Serpents and toads that dwell in mud,
And other creatures with cold blood
That sightless crawl in slime, and sink.
Gadsooks! It makes me sick to think
That man must so exalt his race
By giving dogs a servile place;
Prate of his transcendentalism,
While you save men by mechanism.
And when I told them how you fought
The demons of the storm, and brought
That life-line from the wreck to shore,
And saved those ninety souls or more,
They argued with such confidence –
'Twas instinct, nature, or blind sense.
A *man* could know when he would do it;
You did it and never knew it.

And so, old chap, by what they say,
You live and die and have your day,

7

Like any cat or mouse or weevil
That has no sense of good and evil
(Though sheep and goats, when they have died,
The Good Book says are classified);
But you, being neuter, go to – well,
Neither to heaven nor to hell.

I'll not believe it, Carlo; I
Will fetch you with me when I die,
And, standing up at Peter's wicket,
Will urge sound reasons for your ticket;
I'll show him your life-saving label
And tell him all about that cable,
The storm along the shore, the wreck,
The ninety souls upon the deck;
How one by one they came along,
The young and old, the weak and strong –
Pale women sick and tempest-tossed,
With children given up for lost;
I'd tell him more, if he would ask it –
How they tied a baby in a basket,
While a young sailor, picked and able,
Moved out to steady it on the cable;
And if he needed more recital
To admit a mongrel without title,
I'd get down low upon my knees,
And swear before the Holy Keys,
That, judging by the way you swam,
Somewhere within your line, a dam
Formed for the job by God's own hand,
Had littered for a Newfoundland.

I feel quite sure that if I made him
Give ear to that, I could persuade him
To open up the Golden Gate
And let you in; but should he state
That from your legs and height and speed
He still had doubts about your breed,
And called my story of the cable
"A cunningly devised fable",

8

Like other rumours that you've seen
In Second Peter, one, sixteen,
I'd tell him (saving his high station)
The devil take his legislation,
And, where life, love, and death atone,
I'd move your case up to the Throne.

COME NOT THE SEASONS HERE

Comes not the springtime here,
    Though the snowdrop came,
And the time of the cowslip is near,
    For a yellow flame
Was found in a tuft of green;
    And the joyous shout
    Of a child rang out
That a cuckoo's eggs were seen.

Comes not the summer here,
    Though the cowslip be gone,
Though the wild rose blow as the year
    Draws faithfully on;
Though the face of the poppy be red
    In the morning light,
    And the ground be white
With the bloom of the locust shed.

Comes not the autumn here,
    Though someone said
He found a leaf in the sere
    By an aster dead;
And knew that the summer was done,
    For a herdsman cried
That his pastures were brown in the sun,
    And his wells were dried.

Nor shall the winter come,
    Though the elm be bare,
And every voice be dumb
    On the frozen air;

But the flap of a waterfowl
   In the marsh alone,
Or the hoot of a horned owl
   On a glacial stone.

The Iron Door

(An Ode)

Its features half-revealed in passing gleams
Which had no origin in earthly light,
Half-buried in a shifting mass of gloom
Which had no kinship with the face of night,
It had its station in the cliffs to stand
Against the clamour of eternal storm.
A giant hand
Had wrought it cruciform,
And placed deep shadows on the sunken panels,
Then in ironic jest,
Had carven out the crest
Of death upon the lintel.
Out of some Plutonian cave
It had been brought, and hung
Within its granite architrave.
I saw no latch or knocker on the door;
It seemed the smith designed it to be swung
But once, then closed forevermore.

The noise as of stubborn waters
Came in from a distant tide
To the beat of Time with slow,
Immeasurable stride.
From an uncharted quarter,
A wind began to blow,
And clouds to rise,
And underneath I saw the forms of mortals
Come and go,
And heard their cries, —
Fragments of speech, bewildered pleas,
That rose upon the pauses of the wind,
To hush upon the thunder of great seas.
And I thought what vain credulities
Should lure those human souls before
This vast inexorable door.

A music which the earth has only known
In the drab hours of its emptiness,
Or in the crisis of a fiery stress
Fell on my ear
In broken chord and troubled undertone.
For in this scale were tragic dreams
Awaiting unfulfilled decrees,
Some brighter than the purest gleams
Of seraphic ecstasies;
And some with hopes and fears
Which ran their paling way
Beyond the boundaries of availing prayer,
To dim-illumined reaches where the frore,
Dumb faces of despair
Gazed at their natural mirror in the door.
Then with the intermittent lull
Of wind and the dull
Break of transitory light,
Where rents in the shawl of the darkness
Revealed star-bursts and clouds in flight,
The cries were winged into language,
And forms which were featureless grew
Into the shapes of persons I knew
Who had tasted of life and had died.

Standing, anxious-eyed,
So small against the drift of space,
Enveloped by the gloom,
A boy searched for his father's face,
With that unvoiced appeal,
Which I remember, when he brought
A water-spaniel home one day,
Crushed beneath an engine-wheel;
And could not, by a rational way,
Be fully made to understand
That the mending of a lifeless body lay
Beyond the surgery of his father's hand.

A master mariner
Stood looking at the dull

Outline of a basalt spur,
Which in the fall and lift of fog,
Took on the shape of a gigantic hull.
He was old and travel-stained,
And his face grained
With rebel questionings
Urged with unsurrendered dignity;
For he had lost three sons at sea,
In a work of rescue known
To the high Atlantic records of that year.
Then as the crag took on the heaving motion
Of the fog, and the roar beat in his ear
Of surge afar off, he hallooed
The unknown admiral of the unknown ocean: —

Ahoy! The latitude and longitude?
Within these parts do the stars fail?
Is the sextant in default?
What signals and what codes prevail?
And is the taste of the water salt
About your reefs? Do you bury your dead
In the national folds?
Is the blood of your sailors red
When songs are sung
At the capstan bars? Are davits swung
At a call from the bridge when the night is dark,
And life like wine is spilled at a word to retrieve
The ravage of gales? Do courage and honour receive
On the wastes of your realm, their fair name and title?
As they do at our sea grey altars, — by your leave.

The fog closed in upon the spur,
The moving hull became a rock
Beneath the undulations, and the shock
Of winds from an unknown compass point cut short
The seaman's challenge till that sound again
From the hinter-sea broke through, and the swart
Impress on his face was stirred
By that insurgent flash
It once had known when after the report

13

Of his sons' loss on the High Seas, he had heard
With a throb of pride,
The authentic word
From the Captain's lips,
Of the way the lads had died.

Another form appeared,
One whom I knew so well, – endeared
To me by all the natural ties which birth
And life and much-enduring love impose.
There was no trace
Of doubt or consternation on her face,
Only a calm reliance that the door
Would open and disclose
Those who by swifter strides had gone ahead.
It was the same expression that she wore,
One evening, when with life-work done,
She went to bed,
In the serene belief that she could borrow
Sufficient strength out of the deep
Resources of a final sleep,
To overtake the others by the morrow.

A young man struck against the door
Demanding with his sanguine prime,
If the eternal steward registered
The unrecorded acts of time;
Not for himself insisting, but for one –
A stranger at his side –
For whom he had staked his life,
And on the daring odds had died.
No one had seen this young man go,
Or watched his plunge,
To save another whom he did not know.
Men only guessed the grimness of the struggle,
The body-tug, the valour of the deed,
For both were wrapped in the same green winding-sheet,
And blood-red was the colour of the weed
That lay around their feet.
Life for a life! The grim equivalent

Was vouched for by a sacred precedent;
But why the one who should have been redeemed
Should also pay the price
In the mutual sacrifice,
Was what he wished to know,
And urged upon the iron, blow by blow.

One who had sought for beauty all his days,
In form and colour, symphony and phrase,
Who had looked on gods made perfect by man's hand,
And Nature's glories on the sea and land, —
Now paused and wondered if the Creator's power,
Finding itself without a plan, was spent,
Leaving no relic at this vacant hour,
But a grave-stone and iron monument.

One who had sought for truth, but found the world
Outside the soul betray the one within,
Knew beacon signals but as casual fires,
And systems dead but for their power to spin,
Laid deeply to his heart his discipline,
Looked at the door where all the roadways closed,
And took it as the clench of evidence,
That the whole cosmic lie was predisposed,
Yet faced it with a fine indifference.

From somewhere near the threshold of the door,
A sharp insistent cry,
Above all other notes, arose, —
A miserere flung out to the sky,
Accompanied by a knocking
So importunate,
It might have been the great
Crescendo from the world of human souls,
Gathering strength to assail
The unhearing ears of God, or else to hail
His drowsy warders at the stellar poles.
Then through a rift
In a storm-cloud's eddying,
A greyness as of drift

15

Of winter snow in a belated spring,
Appeared upon a woman's face,
Eroded with much perishing.
The same dark burden under which the race
Reaches old age lay strapped upon her soul: —
That which collects in silence all the shame,
Through hidden passages of time and blood,
Then puts the open stigma of the blame
Upon a spotless name.

Why all the purchase of her pain,
And all her love could not atone
For that incalculable stain:
Why from that tortuous stream, —
Flesh of her flesh, bone of her bone, —
Should issue forth a Cain;
Were queries rained upon the iron plates.
'Twas not enough, it seemed, that her one gift
To life should be returned
To death, but that the Fates
Should so conspire
To have this one devoted offering burned
At such an altar, and by such a fire!
But what availed
A woman's cry against the arrest
Of hope when every rubric paled
Before the Theban mockery of the crest?   2

And at this darkest moment, as I dreamed,
The world with its dead weight of burdens seemed
To pause before the door, in drifts of sand,
And catacombs of rock and burial turf:
For every wind that raged upon the land
Had fled the nescient hollow of God's hand.
And all the music left upon its waters
Lay in the grey rotation of the surf,
With calls of seamen in great weariness
At their unanswered signals of distress;
And all the light remaining was bereft
Of colour and design in full eclipse;

16

No fragrance in the fields; no flowers left
But poppies with their charred autumnal lips.

Then with a suddenness beyond surprise,
When life was sinking in its cosmic trial,
And time was running down before my eyes,
New lights and shadows leaped upon the dial.

I have often heard it said that by some token,
As fragile as a shell,
Or a wish thrice-spoken,
The direst spell,
Though old and ringed of iron, might be broken;
That a fool's belief in the incredible,
Joined to the sounding magic of a name,
Makes up the stuff of miracle.
From such a source, it well might be,
Came this supreme authority.

It may have been the young man's claim
On life; or the old captain calling stormily
From sea to sea;
Or that root faith within a woman's heart;
Perhaps it was the white face of the child;
Or that last argument so wild
Of wing, of such tumultuous breath,
Its strange unreason might be made to prove
The case for life before the throne of death,
I do not know;
But in the dream the door began to move.

A light shot through the narrow cleft,
And shattered into hurrying gleams that rode
Upon the backs of clouds, and through deep hollows,
Like couriers with weird, prophetic code.
And as the door swung forward slowly,
A sound was heard, now like the beat
Of tides under the drive of winds,
Now like the swift deck-tread of feet,
Steadying to a drum
Which marshalled them to quarters, or the hum

17

Of multitudinous voices that would tell
Of the move of life invincible.

Then as the opening widened,
And the sound became more clear, I tried
With an insatiate hunger, to discover
The fountain of that light and life inside;
And with an exultation which outrode
The vaunt of raw untutored strength, I cried; –

Now shall be read
The faded symbols of the page which keeps
This hoary riddle of the dead.

But something heavy and as old as clay,
Which mires a human soul,
Laid hold upon the quest so that it fell,
Just baffled of its goal.
Beyond the threshold of the door,
I could not see; I only knew
That those who had been standing, waiting there,
Were passing through;
And while it was not given me to know
Whither their journey led, I had caught the sense
Of life with high auroras and the flow
Of wide majestic spaces;
Of light abundant; and of keen impassioned faces,
Transfigured underneath its vivid glow.

Then the door moved to its close with a loud,
Relentless swing, as backed by ocean power;
But neither gird of hinges, nor the feel of air
Returning with its drizzled weight of cloud,
Could cancel half the meaning of that hour, –
Not though the vision passed away,
And I was left alone, aware
Of blindness falling with terrestrial day
On sight enfeebled by the solar glare.

Many Moods

THE WAY OF CAPE RACE

Lion-hunger, tiger-leap!
The waves are bred no other way;
It was their way when the Norseman came,
It was the same in Cabot's day:
A thousand years will come again,
When a thousand years have passed away –
Galleon, frigate, liner, plane,
The muster of the slain.

They have placed the light, fog-horn and bell
Along the shore: the wardens keep
Their posts – they do not quell
The roar; they shorten not the leap.
The waves still ring the knell
Of ships that pass at night,
Of dreadnought and of cockle-shell:
They do not heed the light,
The fog-horn and the bell –
Lion-hunger, tiger-leap!

THE MAN AND THE MACHINE

By right of fires that smelted ore
Which he had tended years before,
The man whose hands were on the wheel
Could trace his kinship through her steel,
Between his body warped and bent
In every bone and ligament,
And this "eight-cylinder" stream-lined,
The finest model yet designed.
He felt his lesioned pulses strum
Against the rhythm of her hum,
And found his nerves and sinews knot
With sharper spasm as she climbed

19

The steeper grades, so neatly timed
From storage tank to piston shot –
This creature with the cougar grace,
This man with slag upon his face.

FROM STONE TO STEEL

From stone to bronze, from bronze to steel
Along the road-dust of the sun,
Two revolutions of the wheel
From Java to Geneva run.   1

The snarl Neanderthal is worn
Close to the smiling Aryan lips,   2
The civil polish of the horn
Gleams from our praying finger tips.

The evolution of desire
Has but matured a toxic wine,
Drunk long before its heady fire
Reddened Euphrates or the Rhine.

Between the temple and the cave
The boundary lies tissue-thin:
The yearlings still the altars crave
As satisfaction for a sin.

The road goes up, the road goes down –
Let Java or Geneva be –
But whether to the cross or crown,
The path lies through Gethsemane.

THE HIGHWAY

What aeons passed without a count or name,
Before the cosmic seneschal,
Succeeding with a plan
Of weaving stellar patterns from a flame,
Announced at his high carnival
An orbit – with Aldebaran!   1

And when the drifting years had sighted land,
And hills and plains declared their birth
Amid volcanic throes,
What was the lapse before the marshal's hand
Had found a garden on the earth,
And led forth June with her first rose?

And what the gulf between that and the hour,
Late in the simian-human day,
When Nature kept her tryst
With the unfoldment of the star and flower –
When in her sacrificial way
Judaea blossomed with her Christ!

But what made *our* feet miss the road that brought
The world to such a golden trove,
In our so brief a span?
How may we grasp again the hand that wrought
Such light, such fragrance, and such love,
O star! O rose! O Son of Man?

FROST

The frost moved up the window-pane
Against the sun's advance,
In line and pattern weaving there
Rich scenes of old romance –
Armies on the Russian snows,
Cockade, sword, and lance.

It spun a web more magical,
Each moment creeping higher,
For marble cities crowned the hills
With turret, fane and spire,
Till when it struck the flaming sash,
The Kremlin was on fire.

THE DRAG-IRONS

He who had learned for thirty years to ride
The seas and storms in punt and skiff and brig,
Would hardly scorn to take before he died
His final lap in Neptune's whirligig.

But with his Captain's blood he did resent,
With livid silence and with glassy look,
This fishy treatment when his years were spent —
To come up dead upon a grapnel hook.

THE DEPRESSION ENDS

If I could take within my hand
The rod of Prospero for an hour,
With space and speed at my command,
And astro-physics in my power,
Having no reason for my scheme
Beyond the logic of a dream
To change a world predestinate
From the eternal loom of fate,
I'd realize my mad chimera
By smashing distaff and the spinner,
And usher in the golden era
With an apocalyptic dinner.
I'd place a table in the skies
No earthly mind could visualize:
No instruments of earth could bound it —
'Twould take the light-years to go round it.
And to this feast I would invite
Only the faithful, the elect —
The shabby ones of earth's despite,
The victims of her rude neglect,
The most unkempt and motley throng
Ever described in tale or song.
All the good lads I've ever known
From the twelve winds of sea and land
Should hear my shattering bugle tone

And feel its summoning command.
No one should come who never knew
A famine day of rationed gruel,
Nor heard his stomach like a flue
Roaring with wind instead of fuel:
No self-made men who proudly claim
To be the architects of fame;
No profiteers whose double chins
Are battened on the Corn-Exchange,
While continental breadlines range
Before the dust of flour-bins.
These shall not enter, nor shall those
Who soured with the sun complain
Of all their manufactured woes,
Yet never had an honest pain:
Not these – the well-groomed and the sleeked,
But all the gaunt, the cavern-cheeked,
The waifs whose tightened belts declare
The thinness of their daily fare;
The ill-starred from their natal days,
The gaffers and the stowaways,
The road-tramps and the alley-bred
Who leap to scraps that others fling,
With luck less than the Tishbite's, fed   2
On manna from the raven's wing.

This dinner, now years overdue,
Shall centre in a barbecue.
Orion's club – no longer fable –   8
Shall fall upon the Taurus head.
No less than Centaurs shall be led
In roaring pairs forth from their stable
And harnessed to the Wain to pull
The mighty carcass of the bull
Across the tundras to the table,
Where he shall stretch from head to stern,
Roasted and basted to a turn.
I'd have the Pleiades prepare
Jugged Lepus (to the vulgar *hare*),

Galactic venison just done
From the corona of the sun,
Hoof jellies from Monoceros,
Planked tuna, shad, stewed terrapin,
And red-gut salmon captured in
The deltas of the Southern Cross.
Devilled shrimps, and scalloped clams,
Flamingoes, capons, luscious yams
And cherries from Hesperides;
And every man and every beast,
Known to the stars' directories
For speed of foot and strength of back,
Would be the couriers to this feast —
Mercury, Atlas, Hercules,
Each bearing a capacious pack.
I would conscript the Gemini,
Persuading Castor to compete
With Pollux on a heavy wager,
Buckboard against the sled, that he,
With Capricornus could not beat
His brother mushing Canis Major.
And on the journey there I'd hail
Aquarius with his nets and pail,
And Neptune with his prong to meet us
At some point on the shores of Cetus,
And bid them superintend a cargo
Of fresh sea-food upon the Argo —
Sturgeon and shell-fish that might serve
To fill the side-boards with *hors d'oeuvres*.

And worthy of the banquet spread
Within this royal court of night,
A curving canopy of light
Shall roof it myriad-diamonded.
For high above the table head
Shall sway a candelabrum where,
According to the legend, dwelt a
Lady seated in a chair
With Alpha, Beta, Gamma, Delta,

Busy braiding up her hair.
Sirius, the dog-star, shall be put
Immediately above the foot,
And central from the cupola
Shall hang the cluster – Auriga,
With that deep sapphire-hearted stella,
The loveliest of the lamps, Capella.

For all old men whose pilgrim feet
Were calloused with life's dust and heat,
Whose throats were arid with its thirst,
I'd smite Jove's taverns till they burst,
And punch the spigots of his vats,
Till flagons, kegs and barrels all
Were drained of their ambrosial
As dry as the Sahara flats.
For toothless, winded ladies who,
Timid and hesitating, fear
They might not stand the barbecue
(Being so near their obsequies),
I'd serve purées fresh from the ear
Of Spica with a mild ragout –
To satisfy the calories –
Of breast of Cygnus stiffened by
The hind left leg of Aries,
As a last wind-up before they die.
And I would have no wardens there,
Searching the platters for a reason
To seize Diana and declare
That venison is out of season.
For all those children hunger-worn
From drought or flood and harvest failing,
Whether from Nile or Danube hailing,
Or Yangtze or the Volga born,
I'd communize the total yields
Of summer in the Elysian fields,
Gather the berries from the shrubs
To crown soufflés and syllabubs.
Dumplings and trifles and *éclairs*

5

And roly-polies shall be theirs;
Search as you may, you will not find
One dash of oil, one dish of prunes
To spoil the taste of the macaroons,
And I would have you bear in mind
No dietetic aunt-in-law,
With hook-nose and prognathic jaw,
Will try her vain reducing fads
Upon these wenches and these lads.
Now that these grand festivities
Might start with holy auspices,
I would select with Christian care,
To offer up the vesper prayer,
A padre of high blood – no white
Self-pinched, self-punished anchorite,
Who credits up against his dying
His boasted hours of mortifying,
Who thinks he hears a funeral bell
In dinner gongs on principle.
He shall be left to mourn this night,
Walled in his dim religious light:
Unto this feast he shall not come
To breathe his gloom. No! rather some
Sagacious and expansive friar,
Who beams good-will, who loves a briar,
Who, when he has his fellows with him
Around a board, can make a grace
Sonorous, full of liquid rhythm,
Boom from his lungs' majestic bass;
Who, when requested by his host
To do the honours to a toast,
Calls on the clan to rise and hold
Their glasses to the light a minute,
Just to observe the mellow gold
And the rare glint of autumn in it.

Now even at this hour he stands,
The benison upon his face,
In his white hair and moulded hands,

No less than in his spoken grace.
"We thank thee for this table spread
In such a hall, on such a night,
With such unusual stores of bread,
O Lord of love! O Lord of light!
We magnify thy name in praise
At what thy messengers have brought,
For not since Galilean days
Has such a miracle been wrought.
The guests whom thou hast bidden come,
The starved, the maimed, the deaf, and dumb,
Were misfits in a world of evil,
And ridden hard by man and devil.
The seven years they have passed through
Were leaner than what Israel knew.
Dear Lord, forgive my liberty,
In telling what thou mayst not know,
For it must seem so queer to thee,
What happens on our earth below:
The sheep graze on a thousand hills,
The cattle roam upon the plains,
The cotton waits upon the mills,
The stores are bursting with their grains,
And yet these ragged ones that kneel
To take thy grace before their meal
Are said to be **thy** chosen ones,
Lord of the planets and the suns!
Therefore let thy favours fall
In rich abundance on them all.
May not one stomach here to-night
Turn traitor on its appetite.
Take under thy peculiar care
The infants and the aged. Bestow
Upon all invalids a rare
Release of their digestive flow,
That they, with health returned, may know
A hunger equal to the fare,
And for these mercies, Lord, we'll praise
Thee to the limit of our days."

He ended. The salubrious feast
Began: with inundating mirth
It drowned all memories of earth:
It quenched the midnight chimes: nor ceased
It till the wand of Prospero,
Turning its magic on the east,
Broke on a master charm, when lo!
Answering the summons of her name,
Fresh from the surf of Neptune came
Aurora to the Portico.

THE PRIZE CAT

Pure blood domestic, guaranteed,
Soft-mannered, musical in purr,
The ribbon had declared the breed,
Gentility was in the fur.

Such feline culture in the gads
No anger ever arched her back –
What distance since those velvet pads
Departed from the leopard's track!

And when I mused how Time had thinned
The jungle strains within the cells,
How human hands had disciplined
Those prowling optic parallels;

I saw the generations pass
Along the reflex of a spring,
A bird had rustled in the grass,
The tab had caught it on the wing:

Behind the leap so furtive-wild
Was such ignition in the gleam,
I thought an Abyssinian child
Had cried out in the whitethroat's scream.

LIKE MOTHER, LIKE DAUGHTER

Helen, Deirdre, Héloïse,
Laura, Cleopatra, Eve!
The knight-at-arms is on his knees,
Still at your altars – by your leave.

The magic of your smiles and frowns
Had made you goddesses by right,
Divorced the monarchs from their crowns,
And changed world empires overnight.

You caught the *male* for good or ill,
And locked him in a golden cage,
Or let him out at your sweet will —
A prince or peasant, lord or page.

But do not preen your wings and claim
That when you passed away, the keys —
The symbols of your charm and fame —
Were buried with your effigies.

For, wild and lovely are your broods
That stole from you the ancient arts;
In tender or tempestuous moods,
They storm the barrens of our hearts.

Amy, Hilda, Wilhelmine,
Golden Marie and slim Suzette,
Viola, Claire and dark Eileen,
Brown-eyed Mary, blue-eyed Bett.

Daughters are ye of those days
When Troy and Rome and Carthage burned:
Ye cannot mend your mothers' ways
Or play a trick they hadn't learned.

But whether joy or whether woe —
Lure of lips or scorn of eyes —
We bless you either way we go,
In or out of Paradise.

THE MIRAGE

Complete from glowing towers to golden base,
Without the lineage of toil it stood:
A crystal city fashioned out of space,
So calm and holy in its Sabbath mood,
It might constrain belief that any time
The altars would irradiate their fires,
And any moment now would start the chime
Of matins from the massed Cathedral spires.
Then this marmoreal structure of the dawn,

Built as by fiat of Apocalypse,
Was with the instancy of vision gone;
Nor did it die through shadow of eclipse,
Through clouds and vulgar effigies of night,
But through the darker irony of light.

SILENCES

There is no silence upon the earth or under the earth like
    the silence under the sea;
No cries announcing birth,
No sounds declaring death.
There is silence when the milt is laid on the spawn in the
    weeds and fungus of the rock-clefts;
And silence in the growth and struggle for life.
The bonitoes pounce upon the mackerel,
And are themselves caught by the barracudas,
The sharks kill the barracudas
And the great molluscs rend the sharks,
And all noiselessly –
Though swift be the action and final the conflict,
The drama is silent.

There is no fury upon the earth like the fury under the sea.
For growl and cough and snarl are the tokens of spend-
    thrifts who know not the ultimate economy of rage.
Moreover, the pace of the blood is too fast.
But under the waves the blood is sluggard and has the
    same temperature as that of the sea.

There is something pre-reptilian about a silent kill.

Two men may end their hostilities just with their battle-
    cries.
"The devil take you," says one.
"I'll see you in hell first," says the other.
And these introductory salutes followed by a hail of gut-
    turals and sibilants are often the beginning of friend-
    ship, for who would not prefer to be lustily damned
    than to be half-heartedly blessed?

No one need fear oaths that are properly enunciated, for they belong to the inheritance of just men made perfect, and, for all we know, of such may be the Kingdom of Heaven.

But let silent hate be put away for it feeds upon the heart of the hater.

Today I watched two pairs of eyes. One pair was black and the other grey. And while the owners thereof, for the space of five seconds, walked past each other, the grey snapped at the black and the black riddled the grey.

One looked to say – "The cat,"

And the other – "The cur."

But no words were spoken;

Not so much as a hiss or a murmur came through the perfect enamel of the teeth; not so much as a gesture of enmity.

If the right upper lip curled over the canine, it went unnoticed.

The lashes veiled the eyes not for an instant in the passing.

And as between the two in respect to candour of intention or eternity of wish, there was no choice, for the stare was mutual and absolute.

A word would have dulled the exquisite edge of the feeling,

An oath would have flawed the crystallization of the hate.

For only such culture could grow in a climate of silence, –

Away back before the emergence of fur or feather, back to the unvocal sea and down deep where the darkness spills its wash on the threshold of light, where the lids never close upon the eyes, where the inhabitants slay in silence and are as silently slain.

THE STOICS

They were the oaks and beeches of our species.
Their roots struck down through acid loam
To weathered granite and took hold
Of flint and silica, or found their home
With red pyrites – fools' mistake for gold.
Their tunics, stoles and togas were like watersheds,
Splitting the storm, sloughing the rain.
Under such cloaks the morrow could not enter –
Their *gravitas* had seized a geologic centre
And triumphed over subcutaneous pain.
Aurelius! What direction did you take   1
To find your hermitage?
We have tried but failed to make
That cool unflawed retreat
Where the pulses slow their beat
To an aspen-yellow age.
Today we cannot discipline
The ferments ratting underneath our skin.
Where is the formula to win
Composure from defeat?
And what specific can unmesh
The tangle of civilian flesh
From the traction of the panzers?   2
And when our children cry aloud
At screaming comets in the skies, what serves   8
The head that's bloody but unbowed?
What are the Stoic answers
To those who flag us at the danger curves
Along the quivering labyrinth of nerves?

COME AWAY, DEATH

Willy-nilly, he comes or goes, with the clown's logic,
Comic in epitaph, tragic in epithalamium,
And unseduced by any mused rhyme.
However blow the winds over the pollen,
Whatever the course of the garden variables,
He remains the constant,
Ever flowering from the poppy seeds.

There was a time he came in formal dress,
Announced by Silence tapping at the panels
In deep apology.
A touch of chivalry in his approach,
He offered sacramental wine,
And with acanthus leaf
And petals of the hyacinth
He took the fever from the temples
And closed the eyelids,
Then led the way to his cool longitudes
In the dignity of the candles.

His mediaeval grace is gone –
Gone with the flame of the capitals
And the leisured turn of the thumb
Leafing the manuscripts,
Gone with the marbles
And the Venetian mosaics,
With the bend of the knee
Before the rose-strewn feet of the Virgin.
The *paternosters* of his priests,
Committing clay to clay,
Have rattled in their throats
Under the gride of his traction tread.

One night we heard his footfall – one September night –
In the outskirts of a village near the sea.
There was a moment when the storm
Delayed its fist, when the surf fell
Like velvet on the rocks – a moment only;

34

The strangest lull we ever knew!
A sudden truce among the oaks
Released their fratricidal arms;
The poplars straightened to attention
As the winds stopped to listen
To the sound of a motor drone –
And then the drone was still.
We heard the tick-tock on the shelf,
And the leak of valves in our hearts.
A calm condensed and lidded
As at the core of a cyclone ended breathing
This was the monologue of Silence
Grave and unequivocal.

What followed was a bolt
Outside the range and target of the thunder,
And human speech curved back upon itself
Through Druid runways and the Piltdown scarps,   1
Beyond the stammers of the Java caves,
To find its origins in hieroglyphs
On mouths and eyes and cheeks
Etched by a foreign stylus never used
On the outmoded page of the Apocalypse.

THE DYING EAGLE

A light had gone out from his vanquished eyes;
His head was cupped within the hunch of his shoulders;
His feathers were dull and bedraggled; the tips
Of his wings sprawled down to the edge of his tail.
He was old, yet it was not his age
Which made him roost on the crags
Like a rain-drenched raven
On the branch of an oak in November.
Nor was it the night, for there was an hour
To go before sunset. An iron had entered
His soul which bereft him of pride and of realm,
Had struck him today; for up to noon
That crag had been his throne.

Space was his empire, bounded only
By forest and sky and the flowing horizons.
He had outfought, outlived all his rivals,
And the eagles that now were poised over glaciers
Or charting the coastal outlines of clouds
Were his by descent: they had been tumbled
Out of their rocky nests by his mate,
In the first trial of their fledgeling spins.

Only this morning the eyes of the monarch
Were held in arrest by a silver flash
Shining between two peaks of the ranges –
A sight which galvanized his back,
Bristled the feathers on his neck,
And shot little runnels of dust where his talons
Dug recesses in the granite.
Partridge? Heron? Falcon? Eagle?
Game or foe? He would reconnoitre.

Catapulting from the ledge,
He flew at first with rapid beat,
Level, direct; then with his grasp
Of spiral strategy in fight,
He climbed the orbit
With swift and easy undulations,
And reached position where he might
Survey the bird – for bird it was;
But such a bird as never flew
Between the heavens and the earth
Since pterodactyls, long before
The birth of condors, learned to kill
And drag their carrion up the Andes.

The eagle stared at the invader,
Marked the strange bat-like shadow moving
In leagues over the roofs of the world,
Across the passes and moraines,
Darkening the vitriol blue of the mountain lakes.
Was it a flying dragon? Head,
Body and wings, a tail fan-spread

36

And taut like his own before the strike;
And there in front two whirling eyes
That took unshuttered
The full blaze of the meridian.
The eagle never yet had known
A rival that he would not grapple,
But something in this fellow's length
Of back, his plated glistening shoulders,
Had given him pause. And did that thunder
Somewhere in his throat not argue
Lightning in his claws? And then
The speed – was it not double his own?
But what disturbed him most, angered
And disgraced him was the unconcern
With which this supercilious bird
Cut through the aquiline dominion,
Snubbing the ancient suzerain
With extra-territorial insolence,
And disappeared.

So evening found him on the crags again,
This time with sloven shoulders
And nerveless claws.
Dusk had outridden the sunset by an hour
To haunt his unhorizoned eyes.
And soon his flock flushed with the chase
Would be returning, threading their glorious curves
Up through the crimson archipelagoes
Only to find him there –
Deaf to the mighty symphony of wings,
And brooding
Over the lost empire of the peaks.

THE TRUANT

"What have you there?" the great Panjandrum said
To the Master of the Revels who had led
A bucking truant with a stiff backbone
Close to the foot of the Almighty's throne.

"Right Reverend, most adored,
And forcibly acknowledged Lord
By the keen logic of your two-edged sword!
This creature has presumed to classify
Himself – a biped, rational, six feet high
And two feet wide; weighs fourteen stone;
Is guilty of a multitude of sins.
He has abjured his choric origins,
And like an undomesticated slattern,
Walks with tangential step unknown
Within the weave of the atomic pattern.
He has developed concepts, grins
Obscenely at your Royal bulletins,
Possesses what he calls a will
Which challenges your power to kill."

"What is his pedigree?"

"The base is guaranteed, your Majesty –
Calcium, carbon, phosphorus, vapour
And other fundamentals spun
From the umbilicus of the sun,
And yet he says he will not caper
Around your throne, nor toe the rules
For the ballet of the fiery molecules."
"His concepts and denials – scrap them, burn them –
To the chemists with them promptly."

                                    "Sire,
The stuff is not amenable to fire.
Nothing but their own kind can overturn them.
The chemists have sent back the same old story –
'With our extreme gelatinous apology,
We beg to inform your Imperial Majesty,
Unto whom be dominion and power and glory,
There still remains that strange precipitate
Which has the quality to resist
Our oldest and most trusted catalyst.
It is a substance we cannot cremate
By temperatures known to our Laboratory.' "

And the great Panjandrum's face grew dark –
"I'll put those chemists to their annual purge,
And I myself shall be the thaumaturge
To find the nature of this fellow's spark.
Come, bring him nearer by yon halter rope:
I'll analyse him with the cosmoscope."

Pulled forward with his neck awry,
The little fellow six feet short,
Aware he was about to die,
Committed grave contempt of court
By answering with a flinchless stare
The Awful Presence seated there.

The ALL HIGH swore until his face was black.
He called him a coprophagite,
A genus *homo*, egomaniac,
Third cousin to the family of worms,
A sporozoan from the ooze of night,
Spawn of a spavined troglodyte:
He swore by all the catalogue of terms
Known since the slang of carboniferous Time.
He said that he could trace him back
To pollywogs and earwigs in the slime.
And in his shrillest tenor he began
Reciting his indictment of the man,
Until he closed upon this capital crime –
"You are accused of singing out of key
(A foul unmitigated dissonance),
Of shuffling in the measures of the dance,
Then walking out with that defiant, free
Toss of your head, banging the doors,
Leaving a stench upon the jacinth floors.
You have fallen like a curse
On the mechanics of my Universe.

"Herewith I measure out your penalty –
Hearken while you hear, look while you see:
I send you now upon your homeward route
Where you shall find

Humiliation for your pride of mind.
I shall make deaf the ear, and dim the eye,
Put palsy in your touch, make mute
Your speech, intoxicate your cells and dry
Your blood and marrow, shoot
Arthritic needles through your cartilage,
And having parched you with old age,
I'll pass you wormwise through the mire;
And when your rebel will
Is mouldered, all desire
Shrivelled, all your concepts broken,
Backward in dust I'll blow you till
You join my spiral festival of fire.
Go, Master of the Revels – I have spoken."

And the little genus *homo*, six feet high,
Standing erect, countered with this reply –
"You dumb insouciant invertebrate,
You rule a lower than a feudal state –
A realm of flunkey decimals that run,
Return; return and run; again return,
Each group around its little sun,
And every sun a satellite.
There they go by day and night,
Nothing to do but run and burn,
Taking turn and turn about,
Light-year in and light-year out,
Dancing, dancing in quadrillions,
Never leaving their pavilions.

"Your astronomical conceit
Of bulk and power is anserine.
Your ignorance so thick,
You did not know your own arithmetic.
We flung the graphs about your flying feet;
We measured your diameter –
Merely a line
Of zeros prefaced by an integer.
Before we came
You had no name.

You did not know direction or your pace;
We taught you all you ever knew
Of motion, time and space.
We healed you of your vertigo
And put you in our kindergarten show,
Perambulated you through prisms, drew
Your mileage* through the Milky Way,
Lassoed your comets when they ran astray,
Yoked Leo, Taurus, and your team of Bears
To pull our kiddy cars of inverse squares.

"Boast not about your harmony,
Your perfect curves, your rings
Of *pure and endless light* – 'Twas we
Who pinned upon your Seraphim their wings,
And when your brassy heavens rang
With joy that morning while the planets sang
Their choruses of archangelic lore,
'Twas we who ordered the notes upon their score
Out of our winds and strings.
Yes! all your shapely forms
Are ours – parabolas of silver light,
Those blueprints of your spiral stairs
From nadir depth to zenith height,
Coronas, rainbows after storms,
Auroras on your eastern tapestries
And constellations over western seas.

"And when, one day, grown conscious of your age,
While pondering an eolith,
We turned a human page
And blotted out a cosmic myth
With all its baby symbols to explain
The sunlight in Apollo's eyes,
Our rising pulses and the birth of pain,
Fear, and that fern-and-fungus breath
Stalking our nostrils to our caves of death –
That day we learned how to anatomize
Your body, calibrate your size

*mileage: 1st ed. *mumu's*

And set a mirror up before your face
To show you what you really were – a rain
Of dull Lucretian atoms crowding space,   1
A series of concentric waves which any fool
Might make by dropping stones within a pool,
Or an exploding bomb forever in flight
Bursting like hell through Chaos and Old Night.

"You oldest of the hierarchs
Composed of electronic sparks,
We grant you speed,
We grant you power, and fire
That ends in ash, but we concede
To you no pain nor joy nor love nor hate,
No final tableau of desire,
No causes won or lost, no free
Adventure at the outposts – only
The degradation of your energy
When at some late
Slow number of your dance your sergeant-major Fate
Will catch you blind and groping and will send
You reeling on that long and lonely
Lockstep of your wave-lengths towards your end.

"We who have met
With stubborn calm the dawn's hot fusillades;
Who have seen the forehead sweat
Under the tug of pulleys on the joints,
Under the liquidating tally
Of the cat-and-truncheon bastinades;
Who have taught our souls to rally
To mountain horns and the sea's rockets
When the needle ran demented through the points;
We who have learned to clench
Our fists and raise our lightless sockets
To morning skies after the midnight raids,
Yet cocked our ears to bugles on the barricades,
And in cathedral rubble found a way to quench
A dying thirst within a Galilean valley –
No! by the Rood, we will not join your ballet."

THE DEED

Where are the roadside minstrels gone who strung
Their fiddles to the stirrup cavalcades?
What happened to the roses oversung
By orchard lovers in their serenades?

A feudal dust that draggle-tailed the plumes
Blinded the minstrels chasing cavaliers:
Moonlight that sucked the colour from the blooms
Had soaked the lyrists and the sonneteers.

Where is the beauty still inspired by rhyme,
Competing with those garden miracles,
When the first ray conspires with wind to chime
The matins of the Canterbury bells?

Not in the fruit or flower nor in the whir
Of linnet's wings or plaint of nightingales,
Nor in the moonstruck latticed face of her
Who cracked the tenor sliding up his scales.

We saw that beauty once – an instant run
Along a ledge of rock, a curve, a dive;
Nor did he count the odds of ten to one
Against his bringing up that boy alive.

This was an arch beyond the salmon's lunge,
There was a rainbow in the rising mists:
Sea-lapidaries started at the plunge
To cut the facets of their amethysts.

But this we scarcely noticed, since the deed
Had power to cleanse a grapnel's rust, transfigure
The blueness of the lips, unmat the weed
And sanctify the unambiguous rigour.

For that embrace had trapped the evening's light,
Racing to glean the red foam's harvestings:
Even the seagulls vanished from our sight,
Though settling with their pentecostal wings.

Narrative Poems

Titans

THE CACHALOT

I

A thousand years now had his breed
Established the mammalian lead;
The founder (in cetacean lore)
Had followed Leif to Labrador;
The eldest-born tracked all the way
Marco Polo to Cathay;
A third had hounded one whole week
The great Columbus to Bahama;
A fourth outstripped to Mozambique
The flying squadron of da Gama;   1
A fifth had often crossed the wake
Of Cortez, Cavendish and Drake;   2
The great grandsire – a veteran rover –
Had entered once the strait of Dover,
In a naval fight, and with his hump
Had stove a bottom of Van Tromp;   8
The grandsire at Trafalgar swam
At the *Redoubtable* and caught her,
With all the tonnage of his ram,
Deadly between the wind and water;
And his granddam herself was known
As fighter and as navigator,
The mightiest mammal in the zone
From Baffin Bay to the Equator.
From such a line of conjugate sires
Issued his blood, his lumbar fires,
And from such dams imperial-loined
His Taurian timbers had been joined,   4
And when his time had come to hasten
Forth from his deep sub-mammary basin,
Out on the ocean tracts, his mama
Had, in a North Saghalien gale,   5
Launched him, a five-ton healthy male,

Between Hong Kong and Yokohama.
Now after ninety moons of days,
Sheltered by the mammoth fin,
He took on adolescent ways
And learned the habits of his kin;
Ransacked the seas and found his mate,
Established his dynastic name,
Reared up his youngsters, and became
The most dynamic vertebrate
(According to his Royal Dame)
From Tonga to the Hudson Strait.
And from the start, by fast degrees,
He won in all hostilities;
Sighted a hammerhead and followed him,
Ripped him from jaw to ventral, swallowed him;
Pursued a shovelnose and mangled him;
Twisted a broadbill's neck and strangled him;
Conquered a rorqual in full sight
Of a score of youthful bulls who spurred
Him to the contest, and the fight
Won him the mastery of the herd.

Another ninety moons and Time
Had cast a marvel from his hand,
Unmatched on either sea or land –
A sperm whale in the pitch of prime.
A hundred feet or thereabout
He measured from the tail to snout,
And every foot of that would run
From fifteen hundred to a ton.
But huge as was his tail or fin,
His bulk of forehead, or his hoists
And slow subsidences of jaw,
He was more wonderful within.
His iron ribs and spinal joists
Enclosed the sepulchre of a maw.
The bellows of his lungs might sail
A herring skiff – such was the gale
Along the wind-pipe; and so large

The lymph-flow of his active liver,
One might believe a fair-sized barge
Could navigate along the river;
And the islands of his pancreas
Were so tremendous that between 'em
A punt would sink; while a cart might pass
His bile-duct to the duodenum
Without a peristaltic quiver.
And cataracts of red blood stormed
His heart, while lower down was formed
That fearful labyrinthine coil
Filled with the musk of ambergris;
And there were reservoirs of oil
And spermaceti; and renal juices
That poured in torrents without cease
Throughout his grand canals and sluices.
And hid in his arterial flow
Were flames and currents set aglow
By the wild pulses of the chase
With fighters of the Saxon race.
A tincture of an iron grain
Had dyed his blood a darker stain;
Upon his coat of toughest rubber
A dozen cicatrices showed
The place as many barbs were stowed,
Twisted and buried in his blubber,
The mute reminders of the hours
Of combat when the irate whale
Unlimbered all his massive powers
Of head-ram and of caudal flail,
Littering the waters with the chips
Of whale-boats and vainglorious ships.

II

Where Cape Delgado strikes the sea,
A cliff ran outward slantingly
A mile along a tossing edge
Of water towards a coral ledge,
Making a sheer and downward climb

49

Of twenty fathoms where it ended,
Forming a jutty scaur suspended
Over a cave of murk and slime.
A dull reptilian silence hung
About the walls, and fungus clung
To knots of rock, and over boles
Of lime and basalt poisonous weed
Grew rampant, covering the holes
Where crayfish and sea-urchins breed.
The upper movement of the seas
Across the reefs could not be heard;
The nether tides but faintly stirred
Sea-nettles and anemones.
A thick festoon of lichens crawled
From crag to crag, and under it
Half-hidden* in a noisome pit
Of bones and shells a kraken sprawled.
Moveless, he seemed, as a boulder set
In pitch, and dead within his lair,
Except for a transfixing stare
From lidless eyes of burnished jet,
And a hard spasm now and then
Within his viscous centre, when
His scabrous feelers intertwined
Would stir, vibrate, and then unwind
Their ligatures with easy strength
To tap the gloom, a cable length;
And finding no life that might touch
The mortal radius of their clutch,
Slowly relax, and shorten up
Each tensile tip, each suction cup,
And coil again around the head
Of the mollusc on its miry bed,
Like a litter of pythons settling there
To shutter the Gorgonian stare.

But soon the squid's antennae caught
A murmur that the waters brought –

*half-hidden: 1st ed. half-ridden

50

No febrile stirring as might spring
From a puny barracuda lunging
At a tuna's leap, some minor thing,
A tarpon or a dolphin plunging –
But a deep consonant that rides
Below the measured beat of tides
With that vast, undulating rhythm
A sounding sperm whale carries with him.
The kraken felt that as the flow
Beat on his lair with plangent power,
It was the challenge of his foe,
The prelude to a fatal hour;
Nor was there given him more than time,
From that first instinct of alarm,
To ground himself in deeper slime,
And raise up each enormous arm
Above him, when, unmeasured, full
On the revolving ramparts, broke
The hideous rupture of a stroke
From the forehead of the bull.
And when they interlocked, that night –
Cetacean and cephalopod –
No Titan with Olympian god
Had ever waged a fiercer fight;
Tail and skull and teeth and maw
Met sinew, cartilage, and claw,
Within those self-engendered tides,
Where the Acherontic flood
Of sepia, mingling with the blood
Of whale, befouled Delgado's sides.
And when the cachalot out-wore
The squid's tenacious clasp, he tore
From frame and socket, shred by shred,
Each gristled, writhing tentacle,
And with serrated mandible
Sawed cleanly through the bulbous head;
Then gorged upon the fibrous jelly
Until, finding that six tons lay
Like Vulcan's anvil in his belly,

He left a thousand sharks his prey,
And with his flukes, slow-labouring, rose
To a calm surface, where he shot
A roaring geyser, steaming hot,
From the blast-pipe of his nose.
One hour he rested, in the gloom
Of the after-midnight; his great back
Prone with the tide, and, in the loom
Of the Afric coast, merged with the black
Of the water; till a rose shaft, sent
From Madagascar far away,
Etched a ripple, eloquent
Of a freshening wind and a fair day.

Flushed with the triumph of the fight,
He felt his now unchallenged right
To take by demonstrated merit
What he by birth-line did inherit –
The lordship of each bull and dam
That in mammalian waters swam,
As Maharajah of the seas
From Rio to the Celebes.
And nobly did the splendid brute
Leap to his laurels, execute
His lineal functions as he sped
Towards the Equator northwards, dead
Against the current and the breeze;
Over his back the running seas
Cascaded, while the morning sun
Rising in gold and beryl, spun
Over the cachalot's streaming gloss,
And from the foam, a fiery floss
Of multitudinous fashionings,
And dipping downward from the blue,
The sea-gulls from Comoro flew,
And brushed him with their silver wings;
Then at the tropic hour of noon
He slackened down; a drowsy spell
Was creeping over him, and soon
He fell asleep upon the swell.

III

The cruising ships had never claimed
So bold a captain, so far-famed
Throughout the fleets a master-whaler —
New England's pride was Martin Taylor.
'Twas in this fall of eighty-eight,
As skipper of the *Albatross*,
He bore South from the Behring Strait,
Down by the China Coast, to cross
The Line, and with the fishing done
To head her for the homeward run
Around the Cape of Storms, and bring
Her to Nantucket by the Spring.
She had three thousand barrels stowed
Under the hatches, though she could,
Below and on her deck, have stood
Four thousand as her bumper load.
And so to try his final luck,
He entered Sunda Strait and struck
Into the Indian Ocean where,
According to reports that year,
A fleet had had grand fishing spells
Between the Cocos and Seychelles.
Thither he sailed; but many a day
Passed by in its unending way,
The weather fair, the weather rough,
With watch and sleep, with tack and reef,
With swab and holystone, salt beef
And its eternal partner, duff;
Now driving on with press of sail,
Now sweaty calms that drugged the men,
Everything but sight of whale,
Until one startling midday, when
A gesture in the rigging drew
The flagging tension of the crew.

In the cross-trees at the royal mast,
Shank, the third mate, was breathing fast,
His eyes stared at the horizon clouds,
His heels were kicking at the shrouds,

His cheeks were puffed, his throat was dry,
He seemed to be bawling at the sky.

"Hoy, you windjammer, what's the matter? 10
What's this infernal devil's clatter?"

"She blows, sir, there she blows, by thunder,
A sperm, a mighty big one, yonder."

"Where-a-way?" was Taylor's scream.

"Ten miles, sir, on the looard beam!" 11

"Hard up and let her go like hell!" 12

With heeling side and heady toss,
Smothered in spray, the *Albatross*
Came free in answer to his yell
And corked off seven with a rout
Of roaring canvas crowding her,
Her jibs and royals bellying out,
With studsail, staysail, spinnaker.
The barque came to; the first mate roared
His orders, and the davits swung,
The block-sheaves creaked, and the men sprung
Into the boats as they were lowered.
With oars unshipped, and every sail,
Tub and harpoon and lance in trim,
The boats payed off before the gale,
Taylor leading; after him,
Old Wart, Gamaliel, and Shank —
Three mates in order of their rank.
The day was fine; 'twas two o'clock,
And in the north, three miles away,
Asleep since noon, and like a rock,
The towering bulk of the cachalot lay.

"Two hundred barrels to a quart,"
Gamaliel whispered to Old Wart.

"A bull, by gad, the biggest one
I've ever seen," said Wart, *"I'll bet'ee,*

54

He'll measure up a hundred ton,
And a thousand gallons of spermaceti."

"Clew up your gab!"
                    "Let go that mast!
There'll be row enough when you get him fast."

"Don't ship the oars!"
                        "Now, easy, steady;
You'll gally him with your bloody noise."   13

The four harpooners standing ready
Within the bows, their blades in poise,
Two abaft and two broadside,
Arched and struck; the irons cut
Their razor edges through the hide
And penetrated to the gut.

"Stern all! and let the box-lines slip.
Stern! Sheer!" The boats backed up.
                                    "Unship
That mast. Bend to and stow that sail,
And jam the pole under the thwart."

With head uplifted the sperm whale
Made for the starboard boat of Wart,
Who managed with a desperate swing
To save his skiff the forehead blow,
But to be crushed with the backward swing
Of the flukes as the giant plunged below;
On this dead instant Taylor cleft
His line; the third mate's iron drew,
Which, for the sounding trial, left
But one boat with an iron true, –
The one that had Gamaliel in it.
The tubs ran out, Gamaliel reckoned
Two hundred fathoms to the minute;
Before the line had cleared the second,   14
He tied the drugg and quickly passed
The splice to Shank who made it fast,

55

And with ten blistering minutes gone,
Had but a moment left to toss
It to the fifth boat rushing on
With Hall fresh from the *Albatross*,
Who when his skiff, capsizing, lay
So low he could no longer bail her,
Caught up the end for its last relay,
And flung it to the hands of Taylor.
With dipping bow and creaking thwart,
The skipper's whaleboat tore through tunnels
Of drifting foam, with listing gunwales,
Now to starboard, now to port,
The hemp ran through the leaden chock,
Making the casing searing hot;
The second oarsman snatched and shot
The piggin like a shuttlecock,
Bailing the swamping torrent out,
Or throwing sidelong spurts to dout
The flame when with the treble turn
The loggerhead began to burn.

A thousand fathoms down the lug
Of rope, harpoon, of boat and drugg,
Began, in half a breathless hour,
To get his wind and drain his power;
His throbbing valves demanded air,
The open sky, the sunlight there;
The downward plunging ceased, and now,
Taylor feeling the tarred hemp strand
Slackening that moment at the bow,
Began to haul hand over hand,
And pass it aft where it was stowed
Loose in the stern sheets, while the crew
After the sounding respite threw
Their bodies on the oars and rowed
In the direction of the pull.

"He blows!" The four whaleboats converged
On a point to southward where the bull
In a white cloud of mist emerged –

Terror of head and hump and brawn,
Silent and sinister and grey,
As in a lifting fog at dawn
Gibraltar rises from its bay.
With lateral crunching of his jaw,
And thunderous booming as his tail
Collided with a wave, the whale
Steamed up immediately he saw
The boats, lowered his cranial drum
And charged, his slaughterous eye on Shank;
The mate – his hour had not yet come –
Parried the head and caught the flank
With a straight iron running keen
Into the reaches of his spleen.
The boats rushed in; when Taylor backed,
Gamaliel leaped in and lodged
A thrust into his ribs, then dodged
The wallowing flukes when Hall attacked.
As killers bite and swordfish pierce   16
Their foes, a score of lances sank
Through blubber to the bone and drank
His blood with energy more fierce
Than theirs; nor could he shake them off
With that same large and sovereign scoff,
That high redundancy of ease
With which he smote his enemies.
He somersaulted, leaped, and sounded;
When he arose the whaleboats hounded
Him still; he tried gigantic breaches,   17
The irons stuck to him like leeches;
He made for open sea but found
The anchors faithful to their ground,
For, every surface run, he towed
The boat crews faster than they rowed.
Five hectic hours had now passed by,
Closing a tropic afternoon,
Now twilight with a mackerel sky,
And now a full and climbing moon.
'Twas time to end this vanity –

Hauling a puny batch of men,
With boat and cross-boards out to sea,
Tethered to his vitals, when
The line would neither break nor draw.
Where was his pride, too, that his race
Should claim one fugitive in a chase?
His teeth were sound within his jaw,
His thirty feet of forehead still
Had all their pristine power to kill.
He swung his bulk round to pursue
This arrogant and impious crew.
He took his own good time, not caring
With such persistent foes to crush
Them by a self-destroying rush,
But blending cunning with his daring,
He sought to mesh them in the toil
Of a rapid moving spiral coil,
Baffling the steersmen as they plied
Their oars now on the windward side,
Now hard-a-lee, forcing them dead
Upon the foam line of his head.
And when the narrowing orbit shrank
In width to twice his spinal length,
He put on all his speed and strength
And turned diagonally on Shank.
The third mate's twenty years of luck
Were ended as the cachalot struck
The boat amidship, carrying it
With open sliding jaws that bit
The keel and sawed the gunwales through,
Leaving behind him as he ploughed
His way along a rising cloud,
Fragments of oars and planks and crew.
Another charge and the death knell
Was rung upon Gamaliel;
At the same instant Hall ran foul
Of the tail sweep, but not before
A well directed iron tore
Three feet into the lower bowel.

Two foes were now left on the sea —
The *Albatross* with shortened sail
Was slatting up against the gale;
Taylor manœuvring warily
Between the rushes and the rough
Wave hazards of the crest and trough,
Now closed and sent a whizzing dart
Underneath the pectoral fin
That pierced the muscle of the heart.
The odds had up to this been equal —
Whale and wind and sea with whaler —
But, for the sperm, the fighting sequel
Grew darker with that thrust of Taylor.
From all his lesser wounds the blood
That ran from him had scarcely spent
A conscious tithe of power; the flood
That issued from this fiery rent,
Broaching the arterial tide,
Had left a ragged worm of pain
Which crawled like treason to his brain, —
The worm of a Titan's broken pride!
Was he — with a toothless Bowhead's fate,   19
Slain by a thing called a second mate —
To come in tow to the whaler's side?
Be lashed like a Helot to the bitts
While, from the cutting stage, the spade   20
Of a harpooner cut deep slits
Into his head and neck, and flayed
Him to the bone; while jesters spat
Upon his carcass, jeered and wrangled
About his weight, the price his fat
Would bring, as with the heavy haul
Of the blocks his strips of blubber dangled
At every click of the windlass pawl?
An acrid torture in his soul
Growing with the tragic hurry
Of the blood stream through that widening hole
Presaged a sperm whale's dying flurry —
That orgy of convulsive breath,

Abhorred thing before the death,
In which the maniac threads of life
Are gathered from some wild abysm,
Stranded for a final strife
Then broken in a paroxysm.
Darkness and wind began to pour
A tidal whirlpool round the spot,
Where the clotted nostrils' roar
Sounded from the cachalot
A deep bay to his human foes.
He settled down to hide his track,
Sighted the keels, then swiftly rose,
And with the upheaval of his back,
Caught with annihilating rip
The boat, then with the swelling throes
Of death levied for the attack,
Made for the port bow of the ship.
All the tonnage, all the speed,
All the courage of his breed,
The pride and anger of his breath,
The battling legions of his blood
Met in that unresisted thud,
Smote in that double stroke of death.
Ten feet above and ten below
The water-line his forehead caught her,
The hatches opening to the blow
His hundred driving tons had wrought her;
The capstan and the anchor fled,
When bolts and stanchions swept asunder,
For what was iron to that head,
And oak – in that hydraulic thunder?
Then, like a royal retinue,
The slow processional of crew,
Of inundated hull, of mast,
Halliard and shroud and trestle-cheek,
Of yard and topsail to the last
Dank flutter of the ensign as a wave
Closed in upon the skysail peak,
Followed the Monarch to his grave.

21

The Titanic

The hammers silent and the derricks still,
And high-tide in the harbour! Mind and will
In open test with time and steel had run
The first lap of a schedule and had won.   1
Although a shell of what was yet to be
Before another year was over, she,
Poised for the launching signal, had surpassed
The dreams of builder or of navigator.
The Primate of the Lines, she had out-classed
That rival effort to eliminate her
Beyond the North Sea where the air shots played
The laggard rhythms of their fusillade
Upon the rivets of the *Imperator*.
The wedges in, the shores removed, a girl's
Hand at a sign released a ribbon braid;
Glass crashed against the plates; a wine cascade,
Netting the sunlight in a shower of pearls,
Baptized the bow and gave the ship her name;   2
A slight push of the rams as a switch set free
The triggers in the slots, and her proud claim
On size – to be the first to reach the sea –
Was vindicated, for whatever fears
Stalked with her down the tallow of the slips
Were smothered under by the harbour cheers,
By flags strung to the halyards of the ships.

MARCH 31, 1912

Completed! Waiting for her trial spin –
Levers and telegraphs and valves within
Her intercostal spaces ready to start
The power pulsing through her lungs and heart.
An ocean lifeboat in herself – so ran
The architectural comment on her plan.
No wave could sweep those upper decks – unthinkable!
No storm could hurt that hull – the papers said so.

The perfect ship at last – the first unsinkable,
Proved in advance – had not the folders read so?
Such was the steel strength of her double floors
Along the whole length of the keel, and such
The fine adjustment of the bulkhead doors
Geared to the rams, responsive to a touch,   3
That in collision with iceberg or rock
Or passing ship she could survive the shock,
Absorb the double impact, for despite   4
The bows stove in, with forward holds aleak,
Her aft compartments buoyant, watertight,
Would keep her floating steady for a week.
And this belief had reached its climax when,
Through wireless waves as yet unstaled by use,
The wonder of the ether had begun
To fold the heavens up and reinduce
That ancient *hubris* in the dreams of men,   5
Which would have slain the cattle of the sun,
And filched the lightnings from the fist of Zeus.
What mattered that her boats were but a third
Of full provision – caution was absurd:
Then let the ocean roll and the winds blow
While the risk at Lloyd's remained a record low. 6

THE ICEBERG

Calved from a glacier near Godhaven coast,   7
It left the fiord for the sea – a host
Of white flotillas gathering in its wake,
And joined by fragments from a Behring floe,
Had circumnavigated it to make
It centre of an archipelago.
Its lateral motion on the Davis Strait
Was casual and indeterminate,
And each advance to southward was as blind
As each recession to the north. No smoke
Of steamships nor the hoist of mainsails broke
The polar wastes – no sounds except the grind
Of ice, the cry of curlews and the lore
Of winds from mesas of eternal snow;

62

Until caught by the western undertow,
It struck the current of the Labrador
Which swung it to its definite southern stride.
Pressure and glacial time had stratified
The berg to the consistency of flint,
And kept inviolate, through clash of tide
And gale, façade and columns with their hint
Of inward altars and of steepled bells
Ringing the passage of the parallels.
But when with months of voyaging it came
To where both streams – the Gulf and Polar – met,
The sun which left its crystal peaks aflame
In the sub-arctic noons, began to fret
The arches, flute the spires and deform
The features, till the batteries of storm,
Playing above the slow-eroding base,
Demolished the last temple touch of grace.
Another month, and nothing but the brute
And palaeolithic outline of a face
Fronted the transatlantic shipping route.
A sloping spur that tapered to a claw
And lying twenty feet below had made
It lurch and shamble like a plantigrade;
But with an impulse governed by the raw
Mechanics of its birth, it drifted where
Ambushed, fog-grey, it stumbled on its lair,
North forty-one degrees and forty-four,
Fifty and fourteen west the longitude,
Waiting a world-memorial hour, its rude
Corundum form stripped to its Greenland core.

SOUTHAMPTON, WEDNESDAY, APRIL 10, 1912

An omen struck the thousands on the shore –
A double accident! And as the ship
Swung down the river on her maiden trip,
Old sailors of the clipper decades, wise
To the sea's incantations, muttered fables
About careening vessels with their cables
Snapped in their harbours under peaceful skies.

8

63

Was it just suction or fatality
Which caused the *New York* at the dock to turn,
Her seven mooring ropes to break at the stern
And writhe like anacondas on the quay,
While tugs and fenders answered the collision
Signals with such trim margin of precision?
And was it backwash from the starboard screw
Which, tearing at the big *Teutonic,* drew
Her to the limit of her hawser strain,
And made the smaller tethered craft behave
Like frightened harbour ducks? And no one knew
For many days the reason to explain
The rise and wash of one inordinate wave,
When a sunken barge on the Southampton bed
Was dragged through mire eight hundred yards ahead,
As the *Titanic* passed above its grave.
But many of those sailors wise and old,
Who pondered on this weird mesmeric power,
Gathered together, lit their pipes and told
Of portents hidden in the natal hour,
Told of the launching of some square-rigged ships,
When water flowed from the inverted tips
Of a waning moon, of sun-hounds, of the shrieks
Of whirling shags around the mizzen peaks.   9
And was there not this morning's augury
For the big one now heading for the sea?
So long after she passed from landsmen's sight,
They watched her with their Mother Carey eyes   10
Through Spithead smoke, through mists of Isle of Wight,
Through clouds of sea-gulls following with their cries.

WEDNESDAY EVENING

Electric elements were glowing down
In the long galley passages where scores
Of white-capped cooks stood at the oven doors
To feed the population of a town.
Cauldrons of stock, purées and consommés,
Simmered with peppercorns and marjoram.
The sea-shore smells from bisque and crab and clam

Blended with odours from the fricassees.
Refrigerators, hung with a week's toll
Of the stockyards, delivered sides of lamb
And veal, beef quarters to be roasted whole.
Hundreds of capons and halibut. A shoal
Of Blue-Points waited to be served on shell.
The boards were loaded with pimolas, pails
Of lobster coral, jars of Béchamel,   11
To garnish tiers of rows of chilled timbales
And aspics. On the shelves were pyramids
Of truffles, sprigs of thyme and water-cress,
Bay leaf and parsley, savouries to dress
Shad roes and sweetbreads broiling on the grids.
And then in diamond, square, crescent and star,
Hors d'oeuvres were fashioned from the toasted bread,
With paste of anchovy and caviare,
Paprika sprinkled and pimento spread,
All ready, for the hour was seven!

                                  Meanwhile,
Rivalling the engines with their steady tread,
Thousands of feet were taking overhead
The fourth lap round the deck to make the mile.
Squash racquet, shuffle board and quoits; the cool
Tang of the plunge in the gymnasium pool,
The rub, the crisp air of the April night,
The salt of the breeze made by the liner's rate,
Worked with an even keel to stimulate
Saliva for an ocean appetite;
And like storm troops before a citadel,
At the first summons of a bugle, soon
The army massed the stairs towards the saloon,
And though twelve courses on the cards might well
Measure themselves against Falstaffian juices,
But few were found presenting their excuses,
When stewards offered on the lacquered trays
The Savoy chasers and the canapés.

The dinner gave the sense that all was well:
That touch of ballast in the tanks; the feel

Of peace from ramparts unassailable,
Which, added to her seven decks of steel,
Had constituted the *Titanic* less
A ship than a Gibraltar under heel.
And night had placed a lazy lusciousness
Upon a surfeit of security.
Science responded to a button press.
The three electric lifts that ran through tiers
Of decks, the reading lamps, the brilliancy
Of mirrors from the tungsten chandeliers,
Had driven out all phantoms which the mind
Had loosed from ocean closets, and assigned
To the dry earth the custody of fears.
The crowds poured through the sumptuous rooms and
    halls,
And tapped the tables of the Regency;
Smirked at the caryatids on the walls;
Talked Jacobean-wise; canvassed the range
Of taste within the Louis dynasty.
Grey-templed Cæsars of the world's Exchange
Swallowed liqueurs and coffee as they sat
Under the Georgian carved mahogany,
Dictating wireless hieroglyphics that
Would on the opening of the Board Rooms rock
The pillared dollars of a railroad stock.

IN THE GYMNASIUM

A group had gathered round a mat to watch
The pressure of a Russian hammerlock,
A Polish scissors and a German crotch,
Broken by the toe-hold of Frank Gotch;   12
Or listened while a young Y.M.C.A.
Instructor demonstrated the left-hook,
And that right upper-cut which Jeffries took   18
From Johnson in the polished Reno way.
By midnight in the spacious dancing hall,
Hundreds were at the Masqueraders' Ball,
The high potential of the liner's pleasures,
Where mellow lights from Chinese lanterns glowed

Upon the scene, and the *Blue Danube* flowed
In andantino rhythms through the measures.

By three the silence that proceeded from
The night-caps and the soporific hum
Of the engines was far deeper than a town's:
The starlight and the low wash of the sea
Against the hull bore the serenity
Of sleep at rural hearths with eiderdowns.

The quiet on the decks was scarcely less
Than in the berths: no symptoms of the toil
Down in the holds; no evidence of stress
From gears drenched in the lubricating oil.
She seemed to swim in oil, so smooth the sea.
And quiet on the bridge: the great machine
Called for laconic speech, close-fitting, clean,
And whittled to the ship's economy.
Even the judgment stood in little need
Of reason, for the Watch had but to read
Levels and lights, meter or card or bell
To find the pressures, temperatures, or tell
Magnetic North within a binnacle,
Or gauge the hour of docking; for the speed
Was fixed abaft where under the Ensign,
Like a flashing trolling spoon, the log rotator
Transmitted through a governor its fine
Gradations on a dial indicator.

Morning of Sunday promised cool and clear,
Flawless horizon, crystal atmosphere;
Not a cat's paw on the ocean, not a guy
Rope murmuring: the steamer's columned smoke
Climbed like extensions of her funnels high
Into the upper zones, then warped and broke
Through the resistance of her speed – blue sky,
Blue water rifted only by the wedge
Of the bow where the double foam line ran
Diverging from the beam to join the edge
Of the stern wake like a white unfolding fan.

Her maiden voyage was being sweetly run,
Adding a half-knot here, a quarter there,
Gliding from twenty into twenty-one.
She seemed so native to her thoroughfare,
One turned from contemplation of her size,
Her sixty thousand tons of sheer flotation,
To wonder at the human enterprise
That took a gamble on her navigation –
Joining the mastiff strength with whippet grace
In this head-strained, world-watched Atlantic race:
Her less than six days' passage would combine
Achievement with the architect's design.

9 A.M.

A message from Caronia: advice
From ships proceeding west; sighted field ice
And growlers; forty-two north; forty-nine   14
To fifty-one west longitude. S.S.
"Mesaba" of Atlantic Transport Line
Reports encountering solid pack: would guess
The stretch five miles in width from west to east,
And forty-five to fifty miles at least
In length.

1 P.M.

         Amerika obliged to slow
Down: warns all steamships in vicinity
Presence of bergs, especially of three
Upon the southern outskirts of the floe.

1.42 P.M.

The *Baltic* warns *Titanic*: so *Touraine*;
Reports of numerous icebergs on the Banks,
The floe across the southern traffic lane.

5 P.M.

The *Californian* and *Baltic* again
Present their compliments to Captain.

Thanks.

THREE MEN TALKING ON DECK

"That spark's been busy all the afternoon –
Warnings! The Hydrographic charts are strewn
With crosses showing bergs and pack-ice all
Along the routes, more south than usual
For this time of the year."

                "She's hitting a clip
Instead of letting up while passing through
This belt. She's gone beyond the twenty-two."

"Don't worry – Smith's an old dog, knows his ship,
No finer in the mercantile marine
Than Smith with thirty years of service, clean
Record, honoured with highest of all commands,
'Majestic', then 'Olympic' on his hands,
Now the 'Titanic'.'

              "'Twas a lucky streak
That at Southampton dock he didn't lose her,
And the 'Olympic' had a narrow squeak
Some months before rammed by the British Cruiser,
The 'Hawke'.'

              "Straight accident. No one to blame:
'Twas suction – Board absolved them both. The same
With the 'Teutonic' and 'New York'. No need
To fear she's trying to out-reach her speed.
There isn't a sign of fog. Besides by now
The watch is doubled at crow's nest and bow."

"People are talking of that apparition,
When we were leaving Queenstown – that head showing
Above the funnel rim, and the fires going!
A stoker's face – sounds like a superstition.
But he was there within the stack, all right;
Climbed up the ladder and grinned. The explanation
Was given by an engineer last night –
A dummy funnel built for ventilation."

"That's queer enough, but nothing so absurd

As the latest story two old ladies heard
At a rubber o' bridge. They nearly died with fright;
Wanted to tell the captain – of all things!
The others sneered a bit but just the same
It did the trick of breaking up the game.
A mummy from The Valley of the Kings
Was brought from Thebes to London. Excavators
Passed out from cholera, black plague or worse.
Egyptians understood – an ancient curse
Was visited on all the violators.
One fellow was run over, one was drowned,
And one went crazy. When in time it found
Its way to the Museum, the last man
In charge – a mothy Aberdonian –
Exploding the whole legend with a laugh,
Lost all his humour when the skeleton
Appeared within the family photograph,
And leered down from a corner just like one
Of his uncles."

    "Holy Hades!"

       "The B.M.   15
Authorities themselves were scared and sold
It to New York. That's how the tale is told."
"The joke is on the Yanks."
       "No, not on them,
Nor on The Valley of the Kings. What's rummy
About it is – we're carrying the mummy."

7.30 P.M. AT A TABLE IN THE DINING SALOON

Green Turtle!
    Potage Romanoff!
        "White Star
Is out this time to press Cunarders close,
Got them on tonnage – fifty thousand gross.
Preferred has never paid a dividend.
The common's down to five – one hundred par.
The double ribbon – size and speed – would send
Them soaring."

        70

"Speed is not in her design,
But comfort and security. The Line
Had never advertised it – 'twould be mania
To smash the record of the 'Mauretania'."
Sherry!

     "The rumour's out."

                "There's nothing in it."
"Bet you she docks on Tuesday night."

                    "I'll take it."
"She's hitting twenty-two this very minute."
"That's four behind – She hasn't a chance to make it."
Brook Trout!

       Fried Dover Sole!

              "Her rate will climb
From twenty-two to twenty-six in time.
The Company's known never to rush their ships
At first or try to rip the bed-bolts off.
They run them gently half-a-dozen trips,
A few work-outs around the track to let
Them find their breathing, take the boiler cough
Out of them. She's not racing for a cup."
Claret!

     "Steamships like sprinters have to get
Their second wind before they open up."

"That group of men around the captain's table,
Look at them, count the aggregate – the House
Of Astor, Guggenheim, and Harris, Straus,
That's Frohman, isn't it? Between them able
To halve the national debt with a cool billion!
Sir Hugh is over there, and Hays and Stead.
That woman third from captain's right, it's said,
Those diamonds round her neck – a quarter million!"
Mignon of Beef!

       Quail!

           "I heard Phillips say
He had the finest outfit on the sea;
The new Marconi valve; the range by day,
Five hundred miles, by night a thousand. Three

71

Sources of power. If some crash below
Should hit the engines, flood the dynamo,
He had the batteries: in emergency,
He could switch through to the auxiliary
On the boat deck."

Woodcock *and* Burgundy!
"Say waiter, I said RARE, *you understand."*
Escallope of Veal!

Roast Duckling!

Snipe! *More* Rhine!

"Marconi made the sea as safe as land:
Remember the 'Republic' – White Star Line –
Rammed off Nantucket by the 'Florida',
One thousand saved – the 'Baltic' heard the call.
Two steamers answered the 'Slavonia',
Disabled off the Azores. They got them all,
And when the 'Minnehaha' ran aground
Near Bishop's Rock, they never would have found   16
Her – not a chance without the wireless. Same
Thing happened to that boat – what was her name?
The one that foundered off the Alaska Coast –
Her signals brought a steamer in the nick
Of time. Yes, sir – Marconi turned the trick."

The Barcelona salad; *no,* Beaucaire;
That Russian dressing;

Avocado pear;

"They wound her up at the Southampton dock,
And then the tugs gave her a push to start
Her off – as automatic as a clock."

Moselle!

"For all the hand work there's to do
Aboard this liner up on deck, the crew
Might just as well have stopped ashore. Apart
From stokers and the engineers, she's run
By gadgets from the bridge – a thousand and one
Of them with a hundred miles of copper wire.
A filament glows at the first sign of fire,
A buzzer sounds, a number gives the spot,

A deck-hand makes a coupling of the hose.
That's all there's to it; not a whistle; not
A passenger upon the ship that knows
What's happened. The whole thing is done without
So much as calling up the fire brigade.
They don't need even the pumps – a gas is sprayed,
Carbon dioxide – and the blaze is out."

A Cherry Flan!
                          Champagne!
                                      Chocolate parfait!

"How about a poker crowd to-night?
Get Jones, an awful grouch – no good to play,
But has the coin. Get hold of Larry."
                                          "Right."
"You fetch Van Raalte: I'll bring in MacRae.
In Cabin D, one hundred seventy-nine.
In half-an-hour we start playing."
                                          "Fine."

ON DECK

The sky was moonless but the sea flung back
With greater brilliance half the zodiac.
As clear below as clear above, the Lion
Far on the eastern quarter stalked the Bear:
Polaris off the starboard beam – and there
Upon the port the Dog-star trailed Orion.
Capella was so close, a hand might seize
The sapphire with the silver Pleiades.
And further to the south – a finger span,
Swam Betelgeuse and red Aldebaran.
Right through from east to west the ocean glassed
The billions of that snowy caravan
Ranging the highway which the Milkmaid passed.

9.05 P.M.

"CALIFORNIAN" FLASHING
I say, old man, we're stuck fast in this place,
More than an hour. Field ice for miles about.

"TITANIC"

Say, "Californian", shut up, keep out,
You're jamming all my signals with Cape Race.

10 P.M.

A group of boys had gathered round a spot
Upon the rail where a dial registered
The speed, and waiting each three minutes heard
The taffrail log bell tallying off a knot.

11.20 P.M.

BEHIND A DECK HOUSE

First act to fifth act in a tragic plan,
Stage time, real time – a woman and a man,
Entering a play within a play, dismiss
The pageant on the ocean with a kiss.
Eleven-twenty curtain! Whether true
Or false the pantomimic vows they make
Will not be known till at the *fifth* they take
Their mutual exit twenty after two.

11.25 P.M.

Position half-a-mile from edge of floe,
Hove-to for many hours, bored with delay,
The *Californian* fifteen miles away,
And fearful of the pack, has now begun
To turn her engines over under slow
Bell, and the operator, his task done,
Unclamps the phones and ends his dullest day.

The ocean sinuous, half-past eleven;
A silence broken only by the seven
Bells and the look-out calls, the log-book showing
Knots forty-five within two hours – not quite
The expected best as yet – but she was going
With all her bulkheads open through the night,
For not a bridge induction light was glowing.
Over the stern zenith and nadir met
In the wash of the reciprocating set.
The foam in bevelled mirrors multiplied

17

74

And shattered constellations. In between,
The pitch from the main drive of the turbine
Emerged like tuna breaches to divide
Against the rudder, only to unite
With the converging wake from either side.
Under the counter, blending with the spill
Of stars – the white and blue – the yellow light
Of Jupiter hung like a daffodil.

D-179

"Ace full! A long time since I had a pot."

*"Good boy, Van Raalte. That's the juiciest haul
To-night. Calls for a round of roodles, what?
Let's whoop her up. Double the limit. All
In."* (Jones, heard muttering as usual,
Demurs, but over-ruled.) *"Jones sore again."*

VAN RAALTE (DEALER):
"Ten dollars and all in!

$\qquad\qquad$ *The sea's like glass
To-night. That fin-keel keeps her steady."*

JONES: $\qquad\qquad$ *"Pass."*
(Not looking at his hand.)

LARRY: $\qquad\qquad$ *"Pass."*

CRIPPS: $\qquad\qquad$ *"Open for ten."*
(Holding a pair of aces.) *"Say, who won
The sweep to-day?"*

$\qquad\qquad$ *"A Minnesota guy
With olive-coloured spats and a mauve tie.
Five hundred and eighty miles – Beat last day's run."*

MAC: *"My ten."*

HARRY: (Taking a gamble on his four
Spades for a flush) *"I'll raise the bet ten more."*

VAN R.: (Two queens) *"AND ten."*

JONES: $\qquad\qquad$ (Discovering three kings)
"Raise you to forty" (face expressing doubt.)

75

LARRY: (Looking hard at a pair of nines) *"I'm out."*

CRIPPS: (Flirts for a moment with his aces, flings
His thirty dollars to the pot.)

MAC: (The same.)

HARRY: *"My twenty. Might as well stay with the game."*

VAN R.: *"I'm in. Draw! Jones, how bloody long you wait."*

JONES: (Withholds an eight) *"One."* (And then draws
     an eight.)

CRIPPS: *"Three."* (Gets another pair.)
                              "How many, Mac?"

MAC: *"Guess I'll take two, no, three."* (Gets a third Jack.)

HARRY: *"One."* (Draws the ace of spades.)

VAN R.:   *"Dealer takes three."*

CRIPPS (THE OPENER): (Throws in a dollar chip.)

MAC: (The same.)

HARRY: *"I'll raise
You ten."*

VAN R.: *"I'll see you."*

JONES: (Hesitates, surveys
The chips.) *"Another ten."*

CRIPPS: *"I'll call you."*

MAC: *"See."*

HARRY: *"White livers! Here she goes to thirty."*

VAN R.:   *"Just
The devil's luck."* (Throws cards down in disgust.)

JONES:
"Might as well raise." (Counts twenty sluggishly,
Tosses them to the centre.)
                      "Staying, Cripps?"

CRIPPS: *"No, and be damned to it."*

MAC: *"My ten."* (With groans.)

HARRY:
(Looks at the pyramid and swears at Jones,
Then calls, pitching ten dollars on the chips.)

JONES:
(Cards down.) *"A full house tops the flush."* (He spreads
His arms around the whites and blues and reds.)

MAC:
"As the Scotchman once said to the Sphinx,
I'd like just to know what he thinks,
I'll ask him, he cried,
And the Sphinx – he replied,
It's the hell of a time between drinks."

CRIPPS (WATCH IN HAND):
"Time? Eleven forty-four, to be precise."

HARRY:
"Jones – that will fatten up your pocket-book.
My throat's like charcoal. Ring for soda and ice."

VAN R.:
"Ice: God! Look – take it through the port-hole – look!"

11.45 P.M.

A signal from the crow's nest. Three bells pealed:
The look-out telephoned – *Something ahead,*
Hard to make out, sir; looks like . . . iceberg dead
On starboard bow!

MURDOCH HOLDING THE BRIDGE-WATCH

                   Starboard your helm: ship heeled   18
To port. From bridge to engine-room the clang
Of the telegraph. *Danger. Stop.* A hand sprang
To the throttle; the valves closed, and with the churn
Of the reverse the sea boiled at the stern.
Smith hurried to the bridge and Murdoch closed
The bulkheads of the ship as he supposed,

But could not know that with those riven floors
The electro-magnets failed upon the doors.
No shock! No more than if something alive
Had brushed her as she passed. The bow had missed.
Under the vast momentum of her drive
She went a mile. But why that ominous five
Degrees (within five minutes) of a list?

IN A CABIN:
"What was that, steward?"
                              "Seems like she hit a sea, sir."
"But there's no sea; calm as a landlocked bay
It is; lost a propeller blade?"
                              "Maybe, sir."
"She's stopped."
                  "Just cautious like, feeling her way,
There's ice about. It's dark, no moon to-night,
Nothing to fear, I'm sure, sir."

                              For so slight
The answer of the helm, it did not break
The sleep of hundreds: some who were awake
Went up on deck, but soon were satisfied
That nothing in the shape of wind or tide
Or rock or ice could harm that huge bulk spread
On the Atlantic, and went back to bed.

CAPTAIN IN WIRELESS ROOM:
"We've struck an iceberg – glancing blow: as yet
Don't know extent; looks serious; so get
Ready to send out general call for aid;
I'll tell you when – having inspection made."

REPORT OF SHIP'S CARPENTER AND FOURTH OFFICER:
A starboard cut three hundred feet or more
From foremast to amidships. Iceberg tore
Right at the bilge turn through the double skin: 19
Some boiler rooms and bunkers driven in;
The forward five compartments flooded – mail
Bags floating. Would the engine power avail
To stem the rush?

78

WIRELESS ROOM, FIRST OFFICER PHILLIPS AT KEY:
                    Titanic, C.Q.D.
Collision: iceberg: damaged starboard side:
Distinct list forward. (Had Smith magnified
The danger? Over-anxious certainly.)
The second (joking) – *"Try new call, maybe
Last chance you'll have to send it."*

                                                    S.O.S.

Then back to older signal of distress.

On the same instant the *Carpathia* called,
The distance sixty miles – *Putting about,
And heading for you; Double watch installed
In engine-room, in stokehold and look-out.
Four hours the run, should not the ice retard
The speed; but taking chances: Coming hard!*

THE BRIDGE

As leaning on her side to ease a pain,
The tilted ship had stopped the captain's breath:
The inconceivable had stabbed his brain,
This thing unfelt – her visceral wound of death?
Another message – this time to report her
Filling, taxing the pumps beyond their strain.
Had that blow rent her from the bow to quarter?
Or would the aft compartments still intact
Give buoyancy enough to counteract
The open forward holds?

                              The carpenter's
Second report had offered little chance,
And panic – heart of God – the passengers,
The fourteen hundred – seven hundred packed
In steerage – seven hundred immigrants!
Smith thought of panic clutching at their throats,
And feared that Balkan scramble for the boats.   20

No call from bridge, no whistle, no alarm
Was sounded. Have the stewards quietly
Inform the passengers: no vital harm,
Precautions merely for emergency;

79

Collision? Yes, but nature of the blow
Must not be told: not even the crew must know:
Yet all on deck with lifebelts, and boats ready,
The sailors at the falls, and all hands steady.

WIRELESS ROOM

The lilac spark was crackling at the gap,
Eight ships within the radius of the call
From fifteen to five hundred miles, and all
But one answering the operator's tap.
Olympic twenty hours away had heard;
The *Baltic* next and the *Virginian* third;
Frankfurt and *Burma* distant one-half day;
Mount Temple nearer, but the ice-field lay
Between the two ships like a wall of stone;
The *Californian* deaf to signals though
Supreme deliverer an hour ago:
The hope was on *Carpathia* alone.

ON THE DECKS

So suave the fool-proof sense of life that fear
Had like the unforeseen become a mere
Illusion — vanquished by the towering height
Of funnels pouring smoke through thirty feet
Of bore; the solid deck planks and the light
From a thousand lamps as on a city street;
The feel of numbers; the security
Of wealth; the placid surface of the sea,
Reflecting on the ship the outwardness
Of calm and leisure of the passengers;
Deck-hands obedient to their officers;
Pearl-throated women in their evening dress
And wrapped in sables and minks; the silhouettes
Of men in dinner jackets staging an act
In which delusion passed, deriding fact
Behind the cupped flare of the cigarettes.

Women and children first! Slowly the men
Stepped backward from the rails where number ten,

Its cover off, and lifted from the chocks,
Moved outward as the Welin davits swung.
The new ropes creaking through the unused blocks,
The boat was lowered to B deck and hung
There while her load of sixty stepped inside,
Convinced the order was not justified.

Rockets, one, two, God! Smith – what does he mean?
The sounding of the bilges could not show
This reason for alarm – the sky serene
And not a ripple on the water – no
Collision. What report came from below?
No leak accounts for this – looks like a drill,
A bit of exhibition play – but still
Stopped in mid-ocean! and those rockets – *three!*
More urgent even than a tapping key
And more immediate as a protocol
To a disaster. *There!* An arrow of fire,
A fourth sped towards the sky, its bursting spire
Topping the foremast like a parasol
With fringe of fuchsia, – more a parody
Upon the tragic summons of the sea
Than the real script of unacknowledged fears
Known to the bridge and to the engineers.

Midnight! The Master of the ship presents
To the Master of the Band his compliments,
Desiring that the Band should play right through;
No intermission.

CONDUCTOR: *"Bad?"*

OFFICER: *"Yes, bad enough,*
The half not known yet even to the crew;
For God's sake, cut the sentimental stuff,
The BLUE BELLS *and Kentucky lullabies.*
Murdoch will have a barrel of work to do,
Holding the steerage back, once they get wise;
They're jumpy now under the rockets' glare;
So put the ginger in the fiddles – Zip
Her up."

NUMBER TEN GOES OVER THE SIDE

Full noon and midnight by a weird design   21
Both met and parted at the median line.
Beyond the starboard gunwale was outspread
The jet expanse of water islanded
By fragments of the berg which struck the blow.
And further off towards the horizon lay
The loom of the uncharted parent floe,
Merging the black with an amorphous grey.
On the port gunwale the meridian
Shone from the terraced rows of decks that ran
From gudgeon to the stem nine hundred feet;   22
And as the boat now tilted by the stern,
Or now resumed her levels with the turn
Of the controlling ropes at block and cleat,
How easy seemed the step and how secure
Back to the comfort and the warmth – the lure
Of sheltered promenade and sun decks starred
By hanging bulbs, amber and rose and blue,
The trellis and palms lining an avenue
With all the vista of a boulevard:
The mirror of the ceilings with festoon
Of pennants, flags and streamers – and now through
The leaded windows of the grand saloon,
Through parted curtains and the open doors
Of vestibules, glint of deserted floors
And tables, and under the sorcery
Of light excelling their facsimile,
The periods returning to relume
The panels of the lounge and smoking-room,
Holding the mind in its abandonment
During those sixty seconds of descent.
Lower away! The boat with its four tons
Of freight went down with jerks and stops and runs
Beyond the glare of the cabins and below
The slanting parallels of port-holes, clear

Of the exhaust from the condenser flow:
But with the uneven falls she canted near
The water line; the stern rose; the bow dipped;
The crew groped for the link-releasing gear;
The lever jammed; a stoker's jack-knife ripped
The aft ropes through, which on the instant brought her
With rocking keel though safe upon the water.

THE "CARPATHIA"

Fifteen, sixteen, seventeen, eighteen – three
Full knots beyond her running limit, she
Was feeling out her port and starboard points,
And testing rivets on her boiler joints.
The needle on the gauge beyond the red,
The blow-offs feathered at the funnel head.
The draught-fans roaring at their loudest, now
The quartermaster jams the helm hard-over,
As the revolving searchlight beams uncover
The columns of an iceberg on the bow,
Then compensates this loss by daring gains
Made by her passage through the open lanes.

THE BAND

East side, West side, all around the town,
The tots sang "Ring-a-Rosie"
"London Bridge is falling down",
Boys and girls together . . .

The cranks turn and the sixth and seventh swing
Over and down, the "tiller" answering
"Aye, Aye, sir" to the shouts of officers –
"Row to the cargo ports for passengers."
The water line is reached, but the ports fail
To open, and the crews of the boats hail
The decks; receiving no response they pull
Away from the ship's side, less than half full.
The eighth caught in the tackle foul is stuck
Half-way. With sixty-five capacity,
Yet holding twenty-four, goes number three.

The sharp unnatural deflection, struck
By the sea-level with the under row
Of dipping port-holes at the forward, show
How much she's going by the head. Behind
The bulkheads, sapping out their steel control,
Is the warp of the bunker press inclined
By many thousand tons of shifting coal.

The smoothest, safest passage to the sea
Is made by number one – the next to go –
Her space is forty – twelve her company:
"Pull like the devil from her – harder – row!
The minute that she founders, not a boat
Within a mile around that will not follow.
What nearly happened at Southampton? So
Pull, pull, I tell you – not a chip afloat,
God knows how far, her suction will not swallow."

Alexander's rag-time band . . .
It's the best band in the land . . .

VOICES FROM THE DECK:
"There goes the Special with the toffs. You'll make
New York to-night rowing like that. You'll take
Your death o' cold out there with all the fish
And ice around."
                    "Make sure your butlers dish
You up your toddies now, and bring hot rolls
For breakfast."
                    "Don't forget the finger bowls."

The engineering staff of thirty-five
Are at their stations: those off-duty go
Of their free will to join their mates below
In the grim fight for steam, more steam, to drive
The pressure through the pumps and dynamo.
Knee-deep, waist-deep in water they remain,
Not one of them seen on the decks again.
The under braces of the rudder showing,
The wing propeller blades began to rise,

And with them, through the hawse-holes, water
    flowing –
The angle could not but assault the eyes.
A fifteen minutes, and the fo'c'sle head
Was under. And five more, the sea had shut
The lower entrance to the stairs that led
From C deck to the boat deck – the short cut
For the crew. Another five, the upward flow
Had covered the wall brackets where the glow
Diffusing from the frosted bulbs turned green
Uncannily through their translucent screen.

ON THE "CARPATHIA"

White Star – Cunarder, forty miles apart,
Still eighteen knots! From coal to flame to steam –
Decision of a captain to redeem
Errors of brain by hazards of the heart!
Showers of sparks danced through the funnel smoke,
The firemen's shovels, rakes and slice-bars broke
The clinkers, fed the fires, and ceaselessly
The hoppers dumped the ashes on the sea.

As yet no panic, but none might foretell
The moment when the sight of that oblique
Breath-taking lift of the taffrail and the sleek
And foamless undulation of the swell
Might break in meaning on those diverse races,
And give them common language. As the throng
Came to the upper decks and moved along
The incline, the contagion struck the faces
With every lowering of a boat and backed
Them towards the stern. And twice between the hush
Of fear and utterance the gamut cracked,
When with the call for women and the flare
Of an exploding rocket, a short rush
Was made for the boats – fifteen and two.
'Twas nearly done – the sudden clutch and tear
Of canvas, a flurry of fists and curses met
By swift decisive action from the crew,

Supported by a quartermaster's threat
Of three revolver shots fired on the air.
But still the fifteenth went with five inside,
Who, seeking out the shadows, climbed aboard
And, lying prone and still, managed to hide
Under the thwarts long after she was lowered.

Jingle bells, jingle bells,
Jingle all the way,
O what fun . . .

"Some men in number two, sir!"
                                    The boat swung

Back
        "Chuck the fellows out."
                                    Grabbed by the feet,
The lot were pulled over the gunwale and flung
Upon the deck.
                "Hard at that forward cleat!
A hand there for that after fall. Lower
Away – port side, the second hatch, and wait."

With six hands of his watch, the bosun's mate,
Sent down to open up the gangway door,
Was trapped and lost in a flooded alley way,
And like the seventh, impatient of delay,
The second left with room for twenty more.

The fiddley leading from a boiler room   25
Lay like a tortuous exit from a tomb.
A stoker climbed it, feeling by the twist
From vertical how steep must be the list.
He reached the main deck where the cold night airs
Enswathed his flesh with steam. Taking the stairs,
He heard the babel by the davits, faced
The forward, noticed how the waters raced
To the break of the fo'c'sle and lapped
The foremast root. He climbed again and saw
The resolute manner in which Murdoch's rapped
Command put a herd instinct under law;
No life-preserver on, he stealthily

Watched Phillips in his room, bent at the key,
And thinking him alone, he sprang to tear
The jacket off. He leaped too soon. *"Take that!"*
The second stove him with a wrench. *"Lie there,
Till hell begins to singe your lids – you rat!"*

But set against those scenes where order failed,
Was the fine muster at the fourteenth where,
Like a zone of calm along a thoroughfare,
The discipline of sea-worn laws prevailed.
No women answering the repeated calls,
The men filled up the vacant seats: the falls
Were slipping through the sailors' hands,
When a steerage group of women, having fought
Their way over five flights of stairs, were brought
Bewildered to the rails. Without commands
Barked from the lips of officers; without
A protest registered in voice or face,
The boat was drawn up and the men stepped out
Back to the crowded stations with that free
Barter of life for life done with the grace
And air of a Castilian courtesy.

*I've just got here through Paris,
From the sunny Southern shore,
I to Monte Carlo went ...*

ISIDOR AND IDA STRAUS

At the sixteenth – a woman wrapped her coat
Around her maid and placed her in the boat;
Was ordered in but seen to hesitate
At the gunwale, and more conscious of her pride
Than of her danger swiftly took her fate
With open hands, and without show of tears
Returned unmurmuring to her husband's side;
*"We've been together now for forty years,
Whither you go, I go."*
                    A boy of ten,
Ranking himself within the class of men,
Though given a seat, made up his mind to waive

87

The privilege of his youth and size, and piled
The inches on his stature as he gave
Place to a Magyar woman and her child.

And men who had in the world's run of trade,
Or in pursuit of the professions, made
Their reputation, looked upon the scene
Merely as drama in a life's routine:
Millet was studying eyes as he would draw them   26
Upon a canvas; Butt, as though he saw them   27
In the ranks; Astor, social, debonair,
Waved *"Good-bye"* to his bride – *"See you to-morrow"*,
And tapped a cigarette on a silver case;
Men came to Guggenheim as he stood there
In evening suit, coming this time to borrow
Nothing but courage from his calm, cool face.

And others unobserved, of unknown name
And race, just stood behind, pressing no claim
Upon priority but rendering proof
Of their oblation, quiet and aloof
Within the maelstrom towards the rails. And some
Wavered a moment with the panic urge,
But rallied to attention on the verge
Of flight as if the rattle of a drum
From quarters faint but unmistakable
Had put the stiffening in the blood to check
The impulse of the feet, leaving the will
No choice between the lifeboats and the deck.

The four collapsibles, their lashings ripped,
Half-dragged, half-lifted by the hooks, were slipped
Over the side. The first two luckily
Had but the forward distance to the sea.
Its canvas edges crumpled up, the third
Began to fill with water and transferred
Its cargo to the twelfth, while number four,
Abaft and higher, nose-dived and swamped its score.

The wireless cabin – Phillips in his place,
Guessing the knots of the Cunarder's race.

Water was swirling up the slanted floor
Around the chair and sucking at his feet.
Carpathia's call – the last one heard complete –
Expect to reach position half-past four.
The operators turned – Smith at the door
With drawn incredulous face. *"Men, you have done
Your duty. I release you. Everyone
Now for himself."* They stayed ten minutes yet,
The power growing fainter with each blue
Crackle of flame. Another stammering jet –
Virginian heard "a tattering C.Q.".
Again a try for contact but the code's
Last jest had died between the electrodes.

Even yet the spell was on the ship: although
The last lifeboat had vanished, there was no
Besieging of the heavens with a crescendo
Of fears passing through terror into riot –
But on all lips the strange narcotic quiet
Of an unruffled ocean's innuendo.
In spite of her deformity of line,
Emergent like a crag out of the sea,
She had the semblance of stability,
Moment by moment furnishing no sign,
So far as visible, of that decline
Made up of inches crawling into feet.
Then, with the electric circuit still complete,
The miracle of day displacing night
Had worked its fascination to beguile
Direction of the hours and cheat the sight.
Inside the recreation rooms the gold
From Arab lamps shone on the burnished tile.
What hindered the return to shelter while
The ship clothed in that irony of light
Offered her berths and cabins as a fold?
And, was there not the *Californian*?
Many had seen her smoke just over there,
But two hours past – it seemed a harbour span –
So big, so close, she could be hailed, they said;

She must have heard the signals, seen the flare
Of those white stars and changed at once her course.
There under the *Titanic*'s foremast head,
A lamp from the look-out cage was flashing Morse.
No ship afloat unless deaf, blind and dumb
To those three sets of signals but would come.
And when the whiz of a rocket bade men turn
Their faces to each other in concern
At shattering facts upon the deck, they found
Their hearts take reassurance with the sound
Of the violins from the gymnasium, where
The bandsmen in their blithe insouciance
Discharged the sudden tension of the air
With the fox-trot's sublime irrelevance.

The fo'c'sle had gone under the creep
Of the water. Though without a wind, a lop
Was forming on the wells now fathoms deep.
The seventy feet – the boat deck's normal drop –
Was down to ten. Rising, falling, and waiting,
Rising again, the swell that edged and curled
Around the second bridge, over the top
Of the air-shafts, backed, resurged and whirled
Into the stokehold through the fiddley grating.

Under the final strain the two wire guys
Of the forward funnel tugged and broke at the eyes:
With buckled plates the stack leaned, fell and smashed
The starboard wing of the flying bridge, went through
The lower, then tilting at the davits crashed
Over, driving a wave aboard that drew
Back to the sea some fifty sailors and
The captain with the last of the bridge command.

Out on the water was the same display
Of fear and self-control as on the deck –
Challenge and hesitation and delay,
The quick return, the will to save, the race
Of snapping oars to put the realm of space
Between the half-filled lifeboats and the wreck.

The swimmers whom the waters did not take
With their instant death-chill struck out for the wake
Of the nearer boats, gained on them, hailed
The steersmen and were saved: the weaker failed
And fagged and sank. A man clutched at the rim
Of a gunwale, and a woman's jewelled fist
Struck at his face: two others seized his wrist,
As he released his hold, and gathering him
Over the side, they staunched the cut from the ring.
And there were many deeds envisaging
Volitions where self-preservation fought
Its red primordial struggle with the "ought",
In those high moments when the gambler tossed
Upon the chance and uncomplaining lost.

Aboard the ship, whatever hope of dawn
Gleamed from the *Carpathia*'s riding lights was gone,
For every knot was matched by each degree
Of list. The stern was lifted bodily
When the bow had sunk three hundred feet, and set
Against the horizon stars in silhouette
Were the blade curves of the screws, hump of the rudder.
The downward pull and after buoyancy
Held her a minute poised but for a shudder
That caught her frame as with the upward stroke
Of the sea a boiler or a bulkhead broke.

Climbing the ladders, gripping shroud and stay,
Storm-rail, ringbolt or fairlead, every place
That might befriend the clutch of hand or brace
Of foot, the fourteen hundred made their way
To the heights of the aft decks, crowding the inches
Around the docking bridge and cargo winches.
And now that last salt tonic which had kept
The valour of the heart alive – the bows
Of the immortal seven that had swept
The strings to outplay, outdie their orders, ceased.
Five minutes more, the angle had increased
From eighty on to ninety when the rows
Of deck and port-hole lights went out, flashed back

A brilliant second and again went black.
Another bulkhead crashed, then following
The passage of the engines as they tore
From their foundations, taking everything
Clean through the bows from 'midships with a roar
Which drowned all cries upon the deck and shook
The watchers in the boats, the liner took
Her thousand fathoms journey to her grave.

*   *   *   *   *

And out there in the starlight, with no trace
Upon it of its deed but the last wave
From the *Titanic* fretting at its base,
Silent, composed, ringed by its icy broods,
The grey shape with the palaeolithic face
Was still the master of the longitudes.

Brébeuf and His Brethren

I

The winds of God were blowing over France,
Kindling the hearths and altars, changing vows
Of rote into an alphabet of flame.   1
The air was charged with song beyond the range
Of larks, with wings beyond the stretch of eagles.
Skylines unknown to maps broke from the mists
And there was laughter on the seas. With sound
Of bugles from the Roman catacombs,
The saints came back in their incarnate forms.
Across the Alps St. Francis of Assisi   2
In his brown tunic girt with hempen cord,
Revisited the plague-infected towns.
The monks were summoned from their monasteries,
Nuns from their convents; apostolic hands
Had touched the priests; foundlings and galley slaves
Became the charges of Vincent de Paul;   3
Francis de Sales put his heroic stamp   4
Upon his order of the Visitation.
Out of Numidia by way of Rome,
The architect of palaces, unbuilt
Of hand, again was busy with his plans,
Reshaping for the world his *City of God*.   5
Out of the Netherlands was heard the call
Of Kempis through the *Imitatio*   6
To leave the dusty marts and city streets
And stray along the shores of Galilee.
The flame had spread across the Pyrenees –
The visions of Theresa burning through   7
The adorations of the Carmelites;
The very clouds at night to John of the Cross   8
Being cruciform – chancel, transept and aisle
Blazing with light and holy oracle.
Xavier had risen from his knees to drive   9
His dreams full-sail under an ocean compass.
Loyola, soldier-priest, staggering with wounds   10

93

At Pampeluna, guided by a voice,
Had travelled to the Montserrata Abbey
To leave his sword and dagger on an altar
That he might lead the *Company of Jesus*.
The story of the frontier like a saga
Sang through the cells and cloisters of the nation,
Made silver flutes out of the parish spires,
Troubled the ashes of the canonized
In the cathedral crypts, soared through the nave
To stir the foliations on the columns,
Roll through the belfries, and give deeper tongue
To the *Magnificat* in Notre Dame.
It brought to earth the prophets and apostles
Out of their static shrines in the stained glass.
It caught the ear of Christ, reveined his hands
And feet, bidding his marble saints to leave
Their pedestals for chartless seas and coasts
And the vast blunders of the forest glooms.
So, in the footsteps of their patrons came
A group of men asking the hardest tasks
At the new outposts of the Huron bounds
Held in the stern hand of the Jesuit Order.

And in Bayeux a neophyte while rapt
In contemplation saw a bleeding form
Falling beneath the instrument of death,
Rising under the quickening of the thongs,
Stumbling along the Via Dolorosa.   11
No play upon the fancy was this scene,
But the Real Presence to the naked sense.
The fingers of Brébeuf were at his breast,
Closing and tightening on a crucifix,
While voices spoke aloud unto his ear
And to his heart – *per ignem et per aquam*.
Forests and streams and trails thronged through his mind,
The painted faces of the Iroquois,
Nomadic bands and smoking bivouacs
Along the shores of western inland seas,
With forts and palisades and fiery stakes.

The stories of Champlain, Brûlé, Viel,
Sagard and Le Caron had reached his town –
The stories of those northern boundaries
Where in the winter the white pines could brush
The Pleiades, and at the equinoxes
Under the gold and green of the auroras
Wild geese drove wedges through the zodiac.
The vows were deep he laid upon his soul.
"I shall be broken first before I break them."
He knew by heart the manual that had stirred
The world – the clarion calling through the notes
Of the Ignatian preludes. On the prayers,
The meditations, points and colloquies,
Was built the soldier and the martyr programme.
This is the end of man – *Deum laudet*,
To seek and find the will of God, to act
Upon it for the ordering of life,
And for the soul's beatitude. This is
To do, this not to do. To weigh the sin;
The interior understanding to be followed
By the amendment of the deed through grace;
The abnegation of the evil thought
And act; the trampling of the body under;
The daily practice of the *counter virtues.*
"In time of desolation to be firm
And constant in the soul's determination,
Desire and sense obedient to the reason."

The oath Brébeuf was taking had its root
Firm in his generations of descent.
The family name was known to chivalry –
In the Crusades; at Hastings; through the blood
Of the English Howards; called out on the rungs
Of the siege ladders; at the castle breaches;
Proclaimed by heralds at the lists, and heard
In Council Halls: – the coat-of-arms a bull
In black with horns of gold on a silver shield.
So on that toughened pedigree of fibre
Were strung the pledges. From the novice stage

To the vow-day he passed on to the priesthood,
And on the anniversary of his birth
He celebrated his first mass at Rouen.

April 26, 1625

And the first clauses of the Jesuit pledge
Were honoured when, embarking at Dieppe,
Brébeuf, Massé and Charles Lalemant
Travelled three thousand miles of the Atlantic,
And reached the citadel in seven weeks.
A month in preparation at Notre Dame
Des Anges, Brébeuf in company with Daillon
Moved to Three Rivers to begin the journey.
Taking both warning and advice from traders,
They packed into their stores of altar-ware
And vestments, strings of coloured beads with knives,
Kettles and awls, domestic gifts to win
The Hurons' favour or appease their wrath.
There was a touch of omen in the warning,
For scarcely had they started when the fate
Of the Franciscan mission was disclosed –
News of Viel, delivered to Brébeuf, –
Drowned by the natives in the final league
Of his return at Sault-au-Récollet!

Back to Quebec by Lalemant's command;
A year's delay of which Brébeuf made use
By hardening his body and his will,
Learning the rudiments of the Huron tongue,
Mastering the wood-lore, joining in the hunt
For food, observing habits of speech, the ways
Of thought, the moods and the long silences.
Wintering with the Algonquins, he soon knew
The life that was before him in the cabins –
The troubled night, branches of fir covering
The floor of snow; the martyrdom of smoke
That hourly drove his nostrils to the ground
To breathe, or offered him the choice of death
Outside by frost, inside by suffocation;

96

The forced companionship of dogs that ate
From the same platters, slept upon his legs
Or neck; the nausea from sagamite,   14
Unsalted, gritty, and that bloated feeling,
The February stomach touch when acorns,
Turk's cap, bog-onion bulbs dug from the snow
And bulrush roots flavoured with eel skin made
The menu for his breakfast-dinner-supper.
Added to this, the instigated taunts
Common as daily salutations; threats
Of murderous intent that just escaped
The deed – the prologue to Huronia!

July, 1626

Midsummer and the try again – Brébeuf,
Daillon, de Noüe just arrived from France;
Quebec up to Three Rivers; the routine
Repeated; bargaining with the Indians,
Axes and beads against the maize and passage;
The natives' protest when they saw Brébeuf,
High as a totem-pole. What if he placed
His foot upon the gunwale, suddenly
Shifted an ounce of those two hundred pounds
Off centre at the rapids! They had visions
Of bodies and bales gyrating round the rocks,
Plunging like stumps and logs over the falls.
The Hurons shook their heads: the bidding grew;
Kettles and porcelain necklaces and knives,
Till with the last awl thrown upon the heap,
The ratifying grunt came from the chief.
Two Indians holding the canoe, Brébeuf,
Barefooted, cassock pulled up to his knees,
Planted one foot dead in the middle, then
The other, then slowly and ticklishly
Adjusted to the physics of his range
And width, he grasped both sides of the canoe,
Lowered himself and softly murmuring
An *Ave*, sat, immobile as a statue.

97

So the flotilla started – the same route
Champlain and Le Caron eleven years
Before had taken to avoid the swarm
Of hostile Iroquois on the St. Lawrence.
Eight hundred miles – along the Ottawa
Through the steep gorges where the river narrowed,
Through calmer waters where the river widened,
Skirting the island of the Allumettes,
Thence to the Mattawa through lakes that led
To the blue waters of the Nipissing,
And then southward a hundred tortuous miles
Down the French River to the Huron shore.
The record of that trip was for Brébeuf
A memory several times to be re-lived;
Of rocks and cataracts and portages,
Of feet cut by the river stones, of mud
And stench, of boulders, logs and tangled growths,
Of summer heat that made him long for night,
And when he struck his bed of rock – mosquitoes
That made him doubt if dawn would ever break.
'Twas thirty days to the Georgian Bay, then south
One hundred miles threading the labyrinth
Of islands till he reached the western shore
That flanked the Bay of Penetanguishene.
Soon joined by both his fellow priests he followed
The course of a small stream and reached Toanché,
Where for three years he was to make his home
And turn the first sod of the Jesuit mission.

'Twas ploughing only – for eight years would pass
Before even the blades appeared. The priests
Knew well how barren was the task should signs,
Gestures and inarticulate sounds provide
The basis of the converse. And the speech
Was hard. De Noüe set himself to school,
Unfalteringly as to his Breviary,
Through the long evenings of the fall and winter.
But as light never trickled through a sentence,
Either the Hurons' or his own, he left
With the spring's expedition to Quebec,

Where intermittently for twenty years
He was to labour with the colonists,
Travelling between the outposts, and to die
Snow-blind, caught in the circles of his tracks
Between Three Rivers and Fort Richelieu.

Daillon migrated to the south and west
To the country of the Neutrals. There he spent   15
The winter, fruitless. Jealousies of trade
Awoke resentment, fostered calumnies,
Until the priest under a constant threat
That often issued in assault, returned
Against his own persuasion to Quebec.

Brébeuf was now alone. He bent his mind
To the great end. The efficacious rites
Were hinged as much on mental apprehensions
As on the disposition of the heart.
For that the first equipment was the speech.
He listened to the sounds and gave them letters,
Arranged their sequences, caught the inflections,
Extracted nouns from objects, verbs from actions
And regimented rebel moods and tenses.
He saw the way the chiefs harangued the clans,
The torrent of compounded words, the art
Concealed within the pause, the look, the gesture.
Lacking all labials, the open mouth
Performed a double service with the vowels
Directed like a battery at the hearers.
With what forebodings did he watch the spell
Cast on the sick by the Arendiwans: 16
The sorcery of the Huron rhetoric
Extorting bribes for cures, for guarantees
Against the failure of the crop or hunt!
The time would come when steel would clash on steel,
And many a battle would be won or lost
With weapons from the armoury of words.
Three years of that apprenticeship had won
The praise of his Superior and no less
Evoked the admiration of Champlain.

That soldier, statesman, navigator, friend,
Who had combined the brain of Richelieu
With the red blood of Cartier and Magellan,
Was at this time reduced to his last keg
Of powder at the citadel. Blockade,
The piracy of Kirke on the Atlantic,
The English occupation of Quebec,
And famine, closed this chapter of the Mission.

1629

II

Four years at home could not abate his zeal.
Brébeuf, absorbed within his meditations,
Made ready to complete his early vows.
Each year in France but served to clarify
His vision. At Rouen he gauged the height
Of the Cathedral's central tower in terms
Of pines and oaks around the Indian lodges.
He went to Paris. There as worshipper,
His eyes were scaling transepts, but his mind,
Straying from window patterns where the sun
Shed rose ellipses on the marble floor,
Rested on glassless walls of cedar bark.
To Rennes – the Jesuits' intellectual home,
Where, in the *Summa* of Aquinas, faith
Laid hold on God's existence when the last
Link of the Reason slipped, and where Loyola
Enforced the high authoritarian scheme
Of God's vicegerent on the priestly fold.
Between the two nostalgic fires Brébeuf
Was swung – between two homes; in one was peace
Within the holy court, the ecstasy
Of unmolested prayer before the Virgin,
The daily and vicarious offering
On which no hand might dare lay sacrilege:
But in the other would be broken altars
And broken bodies of both Host and priest.
Then of which home, the son? From which the exile?
With his own blood Brébeuf wrote his last vow –

100

"Lord Jesus! Thou didst save me with thy blood;
By thy most precious death; and this is why
I make this pledge to serve thee all my life
In the Society of Jesus — never
To serve another than thyself. Hereby
I sign this promise in my blood, ready
To sacrifice it all as willingly
As now I give this drop." — Jean de Brébeuf.

Nor did the clamour of the *Thirty Years*,   20
The battle-cries at La Rochelle and Fribourg,
Blow out the flame. Less strident than the names
Of Richelieu and Mazarin, Condé,   21
Turenne, but just as mighty, were the calls   22
Of the new apostolate. A century
Before had Xavier from the Indies summoned
The world to other colours. Now appeals
Were ringing through the history of New France.
Le Jeune, following the example of Biard
And Charles Lalemant, was capturing souls
By thousands with the fire of the *Relations*:   23
Noble and peasant, layman, priest and nun
Gave of their wealth and power and personal life.
Among his new recruits were Chastellain,
Pijart, Le Mercier, and Isaac Jogues,
The Lalemants — Jerome and Gabriel —
Jerome who was to supervise and write,
With Ragueneau, the drama of the Mission;
Who told of the survivors reaching France
When the great act was closed that *"all of them*
Still hold their resolution to return
To the combat at the first sound of the trumpets."
The other, Gabriel, who would share the crown
With Jean Brébeuf, pitting the frailest body
Against the hungers of the wilderness,
The fevers of the lodges and the fires
That slowly wreathed themselves around a stake.

Then Garnier, comrade of Jogues. The winds
Had fanned to a white heat the hearth and placed

Three brothers under vows – the Carmelite,
The Capuchin, and his, the Jesuit.
The gentlest of his stock, he had resolved
To seek and to accept a post that would
Transmit his nurture through a discipline
That multiplied the living martyrdoms
Before the casual incident of death.

To many a vow did Chabanel subject
His timid nature as the evidence
Of trial came through the Huronian records.
He needed every safeguard of the soul
To fortify the will, for every day
Would find him fighting, mastering his revolt
Against the native life and practices.
Of all the priests he could the least endure
The sudden transformation from the Chair
Of College Rhetoric to the heat and drag
Of portages, from the monastic calm
To the noise and smoke and vermin of the lodges,
And the insufferable sights and stinks
When, at the High Feast of the Dead, the bodies
Lying for months or years upon the scaffolds
Were taken down, stripped of their flesh, caressed,
Strung up along the cabin poles and then
Cast in a pit for common burial.
The day would come when in the wilderness,
The weary hand protesting, he would write
This final pledge – *"I, Noel Chabanel,*
Do vow, in the presence of the Sacrament
Of Thy most precious blood and body, here
To stay forever with the Huron Mission,
According to commands of my Superiors.
Therefore I do beseech Thee to receive me
As Thy perpetual servant and to make
Me worthy of so sublime a ministry."

And the same spirit breathed on Chaumonot,
Making his restless and undisciplined soul
At first seek channels of renunciation

102

In abstinence, ill health and beggary.
His months of pilgrimages to the shrines
At Rome and to the Lady of Loretto,
The static hours upon his knees had sapped
His strength, turning an introspective mind
Upon the weary circuit of its thoughts,
Until one day a letter from Brébeuf
Would come to burn the torpors of his heart
And galvanize a raw novitiate.

1633

III
New France restored! Champlain, Massé, Brébeuf
Were in Quebec, hopes riding high as ever.
Davost and Daniel soon arrived to join
The expedition west. Midsummer trade,
The busiest the Colony had known,
Was over: forty-three canoes to meet
The hazards of return; the basic sense
Of safety, now Champlain was on the scene;
The joy of the Toanché Indians
As they beheld Brébeuf and heard him speak
In their own tongue, was happy augury.
But as before upon the eve of starting
The path was blocked, so now the unforeseen
Stepped in. A trade and tribal feud long-blown
Between the Hurons and the Allumettes
Came to a head when the Algonquin chief
Forbade the passage of the priests between
His island and the shore. The Hurons knew
The roughness of this channel, and complied.

In such delays which might have been construed
By lesser wills as exits of escape,
As providential doors on a light latch,
The Fathers entered deeper preparation.
They worked incessantly among the tribes
In the environs of Quebec, took hold
Of Huron words and beat them into order.

Davost and Daniel gathered from the store
Of speech, manners, and customs that Brébeuf
Had garnered, all the subtleties to make
The bargain for the journey. The next year
Seven canoes instead of forty! Fear
Of Iroquois following a recent raid
And massacre; growing distrust of priests;
The sense of risk in having men aboard
Unskilled in fire-arms, helpless at the paddles
And on the portages – all these combined
To sharpen the terms until the treasury
Was dry of presents and of promises.

1634

The ardours of his trip eight years before
Fresh in his mind, Brébeuf now set his face
To graver peril, for the native mood
Was hostile. On the second week the corn
Was low, a handful each a day. Sickness
Had struck the Huron, slowing down the blades,
And turning murmurs into menaces
Against the Blackrobes and their French companions. 25
The first blow hit Davost. Robbed of his books,
Papers and altar linens, he was left
At the Island of the Allumettes; Martin
Was put ashore at Nipissing; Baron   26
And Daniel were deserted, made to take
Their chances with canoes along the route,
Yet all in turn, tattered, wasted, with feet
Bleeding – broken though not in will, rejoined
Their great companion after he had reached
The forest shores of the Fresh Water Sea,
And guided by the sight of smoke had entered
The village of Ihonatiria.

A year's success flattered the priestly hope
That on this central field seed would be sown
On which the yield would be the Huron nation
Baptized and dedicated to the Faith;

And that a richer harvest would be gleaned
Of duskier grain from the same seed on more
Forbidding ground when the arch-foes themselves
Would be re-born under the sacred rites.
For there was promise in the auspices.
Ihonatiria received Brébeuf
With joy. Three years he had been there, a friend
Whose visit to the tribes could not have sprung
From inspiration rooted in private gain.
He had not come to stack the arquebuses
Against the mountains of the beaver pelts.
He had not come to kill. Between the two –
Barter and battle – what was left to explain
A stranger in their midst? The name *Echon* 28
Had solved the riddle

                    So with native help
The Fathers built their mission house – the frame
Of young elm-poles set solidly in earth;
Their supple tops bent, lashed and braced to form
The arched roof overlaid with cedar-bark.
"No Louvre or palace is this cabin," wrote
Brébeuf, *"no stories, cellar, garret, windows,*
No chimney – only at the top a hole
To let the smoke escape. Inside, three rooms
With doors of wood alone set it apart
From the single long-house of the Indians.
The first is used for storage; in the second
Our kitchen, bedroom and refectory;
Our bedstead is the earth; rushes and boughs
For mattresses and pillows; in the third,
Which is our chapel, we have placed the altar,
The images and vessels of the Mass."
It was the middle room that drew the natives,
Day after day, to share the sagamite
And raisins, and to see the marvels brought
From France – marvels on which the Fathers built
A basis of persuasion, recognizing
The potency of awe for natures nurtured

On charms and spells, invoking kindly spirits
And exorcising demons. So the natives
Beheld a mass of iron chips like bees
Swarm to a lodestone: was it gum that held
Them fast? They watched the handmill grind the corn;
Gaped at a lens eleven-faceted
That multiplied a bead as many times,
And at a phial where a captive flea
Looked like a beetle. But the miracle
Of all, the clock! It showed the hours; it struck
Or stopped upon command. *Le Capitaine*
Du Jour which moved its hands before its face,
Called up the dawn, saluted noon, rang out
The sunset, summoned with the count of twelve
The Fathers to a meal, or sent at four
The noisy pack of Indians to their cabins.
"What did it say?" "Yo eiouahaoua –
Time to put on the cauldron." "And what now?"
"Time to go home at once and close the door."
It was alive: an *oki* dwelt inside,
Peering out through that black hub on the dial.

As great a mystery was writing – how
A Frenchman fifteen miles away could know
The meaning of black signs the runner brought.
Sometimes the marks were made on peel of bark,
Sometimes on paper – in itself a wonder!
From what strange tree was it the inside rind?
What charm was in the ink that transferred thought
Across such space without a spoken word?
This growing confirmation of belief
Was speeded by events wherein good fortune
Waited upon the priestly word and act.

Aug. 27, 1635

A moon eclipse was due – Brébeuf had known it –
Had told the Indians of the moment when
The shadow would be thrown across the face.
Nor was there wastage in the prayers as night,

Uncurtained by a single cloud, produced
An orb most perfect. No one knew the lair
Or nest from which the shadow came; no one
The home to which it travelled when it passed.
Only the vague uncertainties were left –
Was it the dread invasion from the south?
Such portent was the signal for the braves
To mass themselves outside the towns and shoot
Their multitudes of arrows at the sky
And fling their curses at the Iroquois.
Like a crow's wing it hovered, broodily
Brushing the face – five hours from rim to rim
While midnight darkness stood upon the land.
This was prediction baffling all their magic.
Again, when weeks of drought had parched the land
And burned the corn, when dancing sorcerers
Brought out their tortoise shells, climbed on the roofs,
Clanging their invocation to the Bird
Of Thunder to return, day after day,
Without avail, the priests formed their processions,
Put on their surplices above their robes,
And the Bird of Thunder came with heavy rain,
Released by the nine masses at Saint Joseph.

Nor were the village warriors slow to see
The value of the Frenchmen's strategy
In war. Returning from the eastern towns,
They told how soldiers had rebuilt the forts,
And strengthened them with corner bastions
Where through the embrasures enfilading fire
Might flank the Iroquois bridging the ditches,
And scaling ramparts. Here was argument
That pierced the thickest prejudice of brain
And heart, allaying panic ever present,
When with the first news of the hated foe
From scouts and hunters, women with their young
Fled to the dubious refuge of the forest
From terror blacker than a pestilence.
On such a soil tilled by those skilful hands

Those passion flowers and lilies of the East,
The *Aves* and the *Paternosters* bloomed.
The *Credos* and the *Thou-shalt-nots* were turned
By Daniel into simple Huron rhymes
And taught to children, and when points of faith
Were driven hard against resistant rock,
The Fathers found the softer crevices
Through deeds which readily the Indian mind
Could grasp – where hands were never put to blows
Nor the swift tongues used for recrimination.

Acceptance of the common lot was part
Of the original vows. But that the priests
Who were to come should not misread the text,
Brébeuf prepared a sermon on the theme
Of Patience: – *"Fathers, Brothers, under call
Of God! Take care that you foresee the perils,
Labours and hardships of this Holy Mission.
You must sincerely love the savages
As brothers ransomed by the blood of Christ.
All things must be endured. To win their hearts
You must perform the smallest services.
Provide a tinder-box or burning mirror
To light their fires. Fetch wood and water for them;
And when embarking never let them wait
For you; tuck up your habits, keep them dry
To avoid water and sand in their canoes. Carry
Your load on portages. Always appear
Cheerful – their memories are good for faults.
Constrain yourselves to eat their sagamite
The way that they prepare it, tasteless, dirty."*

And by the priests upon the ground all dots
And commas were observed. They suffered smoke
That billowed from the back-draughts at the roof,
Smothered the cabin, seared the eyes; the fire
That broiled the face, while frost congealed the spine;
The food from unwashed platters where refusal
Was an offence; the rasp of speech maintained
All day by men who never learned to talk

In quiet tones; the drums of the Diviners
Blasting the night – all this without complaint!
And more – whatever sleep was possible
To snatch from the occasional lull of cries
Was broken by uncovenanted fleas
That fastened on the priestly flesh like hornets.
Carving the curves of favour on the lips,
Tailoring the man into the Jesuit coat,
Wrapping the smiles round inward maledictions,
And sublimating hoary Gallic oaths
Into the *Benedicite* when dogs
And squaws and reeking children violated
The hours of rest, were penances unnamed
Within the iron code of good Ignatius.
Was there a limit of obedience
Outside the jurisdiction of this Saint?
How often did the hand go up to lower
The flag? How often by some ringing order
Was it arrested at the halliard touch?
How often did Brébeuf seal up his ears
When blows and insults woke ancestral fifes
Within his brain, blood-cells, and viscera,
Is not explicit in the written story.

But never could the Indians infer
Self-gain or anything but simple courage
Inspired by a zeal beyond reproof,
As when the smallpox spreading like a flame
Destroying hundreds, scarifying thousands,
The Fathers took their chances of contagion,
Their broad hats warped by rain, their moccasins
Worn to the kibes, that they might reach the huts,   30
Share with the sick their dwindled stock of food –
A sup of partridge broth or raisin juice,
Inscribe the sacred sign of the cross, and place
A touch of moisture from the Holy Water
Upon the forehead of a dying child.

Before the year was gone the priests were shown
The way the Hurons could prepare for death

A captive foe. The warriors had surprised
A band of Iroquois and had reserved
The one survivor for a fiery pageant.
No cunning of an ancient Roman triumph,
Nor torment of a Medici confession
Surpassed the subtle savagery of art
Which made the dressing for the sacrifice
A ritual of mockery for the victim.
What visions of the past came to Brébeuf,
And what forebodings of the days to come,
As he beheld this weird compound of life
In jest and intent taking place before
His eyes – the crude unconscious variants
Of reed and sceptre, robe and cross, brier
And crown! Might not one day baptismal drops
Be turned against him in a rain of death?
Whatever the appeals made by the priests,
They could not break the immemorial usage
Or vary one detail. The prisoner
Was made to sing his death-song, was embraced,
Hailed with ironic greetings, forced to state
His willingness to die.

                    *"See how your hands
Are crushed. You cannot thus desire to live.
No.*

    Then be of good courage – you shall die.
True! – What shall be the manner of my death?
By fire.

        When shall it be?

                    Tonight.

                            What hour?

At sunset.

        All is well."

                    Eleven fires
Were lit along the whole length of the cabin.
His body smeared with pitch and bound with belts
Of bark, the Iroquois was forced to run
The fires, stopped at each end by the young braves,

110

And swiftly driven back, and when he swooned,
They carried him outside to the night air,
Laid him on fresh damp moss, poured cooling water
Into his mouth, and to his burns applied
The soothing balsams. With resuscitation
They lavished on him all the courtesies
Of speech and gesture, gave him food and drink,
Compassionately spoke of his wounds and pain.
The ordeal every hour was resumed
And halted, but, with each recurrence, blows
Were added to the burns and gibes gave place
To yells until the sacrificial dawn,
Lighting the scaffold, dimming the red glow
Of the hatchet collar, closed the festival.   32

Brébeuf had seen the worst. He knew that when
A winter pack of wolves brought down a stag
There was no waste of time between the leap
And the business click upon the jugular.
Such was the forthright honesty in death
Among the brutes. They had not learned the sport
Of dallying around the nerves to halt
A quick despatch. A human art was torture,
Where Reason crept into the veins, mixed tar
With blood and brewed its own intoxicant.
Brébeuf had pleaded for the captive's life,
But as the night wore on, would not his heart,
Colliding with his mind, have wished for death?
The plea refused, he gave the Iroquois
The only consolation in his power.
He went back to his cabin, heavy in heart.
To stem that viscous melanotic current
Demanded labour, time, and sacrifice.
Those passions were not altered over-night.
Two plans were in his mind – the one concerned
The seminary started in Quebec.
The children could be sent there to be trained
In Christian precepts, weaned from superstition
And from the savage spectacle of death.

111

He saw the way the women and their broods
Danced round the scaffold in their exaltation.
How much of this was habit and how much
Example? Curiously Brébeuf revolved
The facets of the Indian character.
A fighting courage equal to the French –
It could be lifted to crusading heights
By a battle speech. Endurance was a code
Among the braves, and impassivity.
Their women wailing at the Feast of Death,
The men sat silent, heads bowed to the knees.
"Never in nine years with but one exception,"
Wrote Ragueneau, *"did I see an Indian weep
For grief."* Only the fires evoked the cries,
And these like scalps were triumphs for the captors.
But then their charity and gentleness
To one another and to strangers gave
A balance to the picture. Fugitives
From villages destroyed found instant welcome
To the last communal share of food and land.
Brébeuf's stay at Toanché gave him proof
Of how the Huron nature could respond
To kindness. But last night upon that scaffold!
Could that be scoured from the heart? Why not
Try out the nurture plan upon the children
And send the boys east, shepherded by Daniel?

The other need was urgent – labourers!
The villages were numerous and were spread
Through such a vast expanse of wilderness
And shore. Only a bell with a bronze throat
Must summon missionaries to these fields.
With the last cry of the captive in his ears,
Brébeuf strode from his cabin to the woods
To be alone. He found his tabernacle
Within a grove, picked up a stone flat-faced,
And going to a cedar-crotch, he jammed
It in, and on this table wrote his letter.
"Herein I show you what you have to suffer.

112

I shall say nothing of the voyage – that
You know already. If you have the courage
To try it, that is only the beginning,
For when after a month of river travel
You reach our village, we can offer you
The shelter of a cabin lowlier
Than any hovel you have seen in France.
As tired as you may be, only a mat
Laid on the ground will be your bed. Your food
May be for weeks a gruel of crushed corn
That has the look and smell of mortar paste.
This country is the breeding place of vermin.
Sandflies, mosquitoes haunt the summer months.
In France you may have been a theologian,
A scholar, master, preacher, but out here
You must attend a savage school; for months
Will pass before you learn even to lisp
The language. Here barbarians shall be
Your Aristotle and Saint Thomas. Mute
Before those teachers you shall take your lessons.
What of the winter? Half the year is winter.
Inside your cabins will be smoke so thick
You may not read your Breviary for days.
Around your fireplace at mealtime arrive
The uninvited guests with whom you share
Your stint of food. And in the fall and winter,
You tramp unbeaten trails to reach the missions,
Carrying your luggage on your back. Your life
Hangs by a thread. Of all calamities
You are the cause – the scarcity of game,
A fire, famine or an epidemic.
There are no natural reasons for a drought
And for the earth's sterility. You are
The reasons, and at any time a savage
May burn your cabin down or split your head.
I tell you of the enemies that live
Among our Huron friends. I have not told
You of the Iroquois our constant foes.
Only a week ago in open fight

They killed twelve of our men at Contarea,
A day's march from the village where we live.
Treacherous and stealthy in their ambuscades,
They terrorize the country, for the Hurons
Are very slothful in defence, never
On guard and always seeking flight for safety.

"Wherein the gain, you ask, of this acceptance?
There is no gain but this — that what you suffer
Shall be of God: your loneliness in travel
Will be relieved by angels overhead;
Your silence will be sweet for you will learn
How to commune with God; rapids and rocks
Are easier than the steeps of Calvary.
There is a consolation in your hunger
And in abandonment upon the road,
For once there was a greater loneliness
And deeper hunger. As regards the soul
There are no dangers here, with means of grace
At every turn, for if we go outside
Our cabin, is not heaven over us?
No buildings block the clouds. We say our prayers
Freely before a noble oratory.
Here is the place to practise faith and hope
And charity where human art has brought
No comforts, where we strive to bring to God
A race so unlike men that we must live
Daily expecting murder at their hands,
Did we not open up the skies or close
Them at command, giving them sun or rain.
So if despite these trials you are ready
To share our labours, come; for you will find
A consolation in the cross that far outweighs
Its burdens. Though in many an hour your soul
Will echo — 'Why hast Thou forsaken me?',
Yet evening will descend upon you when,
Your heart too full of holy exultation,
You call like Xavier — 'Enough, O Lord!' "

This letter was to loom in history,
For like a bulletin it would be read

In France, and men whose bones were bound for dust
Would find that on those jagged characters
Their names would rise from their oblivion
To flame on an eternal Calendar.
Already to the field two young recruits
Had come – Pijart, Le Mercier; on their way
Were Chastellain with Garnier and Jogues
Followed by Ragueneau and Du Peron.

On many a night in lonely intervals,
The priest would wander to the pines and build
His oratory where celestial visions
Sustained his soul. As unto Paul and John
Of Patmos and the martyr multitude
The signs were given – voices from the clouds,
Forms that illumined darkness, stabbed despair,
Turned dungeons into temples and a brand
Of shame into the ultimate boast of time –
So to Brébeuf had Christ appeared and Mary.
One night at prayer he heard a voice command –
"*Rise, Read!*" Opening the *Imitatio Christi*,
His eyes "*without design*" fell on the chapter,
Concerning the royal way of the Holy Cross,
Which placed upon his spirit "*a great peace*".
And then, day having come, he wrote his vow –
"*My God, my Saviour, I take from thy hand
The cup of thy sufferings. I invoke thy name;
I vow never to fail thee in the grace
Of martyrdom, if by thy mercy, Thou
Dost offer it to me. I bind myself,
And when I have received the stroke of death,
I will accept it from thy gracious hand
With all pleasure and with joy in my heart;
To thee my blood, my body and my life.*"

IV
The labourers were soon put to their tasks, –
The speech, the founding of new posts, the sick:
Ihonatiria, a phantom town,
Through plague and flight abandoned as a base,
The Fathers chose the site, Teanaostayé,

To be the second mission of St. Joseph.
But the prime hope was on Ossossané,
A central town of fifty cabins built
On the east shore of Nottawasaga Bay.
The native council had approved the plans.
The presence of the priests with their lay help
Would be defence against the Iroquois.
Under the supervision of Pijart
The place was fortified, ramparts were strengthened,
And towers of heavy posts set at the angles.
And in the following year the artisans
And labourers from Quebec with Du Peron,
Using broad-axe and whipsaw built a church,
The first one in the whole Huronian venture
To be of wood. Close to their lodge, the priests
Dug up the soil and harrowed it to plant
A mere handful of wheat from which they raised
A half a bushel for the altar bread.
From the wild grapes they made a cask of wine
For the Holy Sacrifice. But of all work
The hardest was instruction. It was easy
To strike the Huron sense with sound and colour –
The ringing of a bell; the litanies
And chants; the surplices worn on the cassocks;
The burnished ornaments around the altar;
The pageant of the ceremonial.
But to drive home the ethics taxed the brain
To the limit of its ingenuity.
Brébeuf had felt the need to vivify
His three main themes of God and Paradise
And Hell. The Indian mind had let the cold
Abstractions fall: the allegories failed
To quicken up the logic. Garnier
Proposed the colours for the homilies.
The closest student of the Huron mind,
He had observed the fears and prejudices
Haunting the shadows of their racial past;
Had seen the flaws in Brébeuf's *points*; had heard
The Indian comments on the moral law

116

And on the Christian scheme of Paradise.
Would Iroquois be there? Yes, if baptized.
Would there be hunting of the deer and beaver?
No. Then starvation. War? And Feasts? Tobacco?
No. Garnier saw disgust upon their faces,
And sent appeals to France for pictures – one
Only of souls in bliss: of *âmes damnées*
Many and various – the horned Satan,
His mastiff jaws champing the head of Judas;
The plummet fall of the unbaptized pursued
By demons with their fiery forks; the lick
Of flames upon a naked Saracen;
Dragons with scarlet tongues and writhing serpents
In ambush by the charcoal avenues
Just ready at the Judgment word to wreak
Vengeance upon the unregenerate.
The negative unapprehended forms
Of Heaven lost in the dim canvas oils
Gave way to glows from brazier pitch that lit
The visual affirmatives of Hell.

Despite the sorcerers who laid the blame
Upon the French for all their ills – the plague,
The drought, the Iroquois – the Fathers counted
Baptisms by the hundreds, infants, children
And aged at the point of death. Adults
In health were more intractable, but here
The spade had entered soil in the conversion
Of a Huron in full bloom and high in power
And counsel, Tsiouendaentaha
Whose Christian name – to aid the tongue – was Peter.
Being the first, he was the Rock on which
The priests would build their Church. He was baptized
With all the pomp transferable from France
Across four thousand miles combined with what
A sky and lake could offer, and a forest
Strung to the *aubade* of the orioles.   34
The wooden chapel was their Rheims Cathedral.
In stole and surplice Lalemant intoned –

"If therefore thou wilt enter into life,
Keep the commandments. Thou shalt love the Lord
Thy God with all thy heart, with all thy soul,
With all thy might, and thy neighbour as thyself."
With salt and water and the holy chrism,
And through the signs made on his breast and forehead
The Huron was exorcised, sanctified,
And made the temple of the Living God.

The holy rite was followed by the Mass
Before the motliest auditory known
In the annals of worship, Oblates from Quebec,
Blackrobes, mechanics, soldiers, labourers,
With almost half the village packed inside,
Or jammed with craning necks outside the door.
The warriors lean, lithe, and elemental,
"As naked as your hand" but for a skin   35
Thrown loosely on their shoulders, with their hair
Erect, boar-brushed, matted, glued with the oil
Of sunflower larded thickly with bear's grease;
Papooses yowling on their mothers' backs,
The squatting hags, suspicion in their eyes,
Their nebulous minds relating in some way
The smoke and aromatics of the censer,
The candles, crucifix and Latin murmurs
With vapours, sounds and colours of the Judgment.

(THE FOUNDING OF FORT SAINTE MARIE)

1639

V

The migrant habits of the Indians
With their desertion of the villages
Through pressure of attack or want of food
Called for a central site where undisturbed
The priests with their attendants might pursue
Their culture, gather strength from their devotions,
Map out the territory, plot the routes,
Collate their weekly notes and write their letters.
The roll was growing – priests and colonists,

118

Lay brothers offering services for life.
For on the ground or on their way to place
Themselves at the command of Lalemant,
Superior, were Claude Pijart, Poncet,
Le Moyne, Charles Raymbault, René Menard
And Joseph Chaumonot: as oblates came
Le Coq, Christophe Reynaut, Charles Boivin,
Couture and Jean Guérin. And so to house
Them all the Residence – Fort Sainte Marie!   36
Strategic as a base for trade or war
The site received the approval of Quebec,
Was ratified by Richelieu who saw
Commerce and exploration pushing west,
Fulfilling the long vision of Champlain –
"Greater New France beyond those inland seas."   37
The fort was built, two hundred feet by ninety,
Upon the right bank of the River Wye:
Its north and eastern sides of masonry,
Its south and west of double palisades,
And skirted by a moat, ran parallel
To stream and lake. Square bastions at the corners,
Watch-towers with magazines and sleeping posts,
Commanded forest edges and canoes
That furtively came up the Matchedash,
And on each bastion was placed a cross.
Inside, the Fathers built their dwelling house,
No longer the bark cabin with the smoke
Ill-trained to work its exit through the roof,
But plank and timber – at each end a chimney
Of lime and granite field-stone. Rude it was
But clean, capacious, full of twilight calm.
Across the south canal fed by the river,
Ringed by another palisade were buildings
Offering retreat to Indian fugitives
Whenever war and famine scourged the land.

The plans were supervised by Lalemant,
Assigning zones of work to every priest.
He made a census of the Huron nation;

Some thirty villages – twelve thousand persons.
Nor was this all: the horizon opened out
On larger fields. To south and west were spread
The unknown tribes – the Petuns and the Neutrals.

(THE MISSION OF THE PETUNS AND NEUTRALS)
1640-1641

VI

In late November Jogues and Garnier
Set out on snow-obliterated trails
Towards the Blue Hills south of the Nottawasaga,
A thirty mile journey through a forest
Without a guide. They carried on their backs
A blanket with the burden of the altar.
All day confronting swamps with fallen logs,
Tangles of tamarack and juniper,
They made detours to avoid the deep ravines
And swollen creeks. Retreating and advancing,
Ever in hope their tread was towards the south,
Until, "*surprised by night in a fir grove*",
They took an hour with flint and steel to nurse
A fire from twigs, birch rind and needles of pine;
And flinging down some branches on the snow,
They offered thanks to God, lay down and slept.
Morning – the packs reshouldered and the tramp
Resumed, the stumble over mouldering trunks
Of pine and oak, the hopeless search for trails,
Till after dusk with cassocks torn and "*nothing
To eat all day save each a morsel of bread*",
They saw the smoke of the first Indian village.

And now began a labour which for faith
And triumph of the spirit over failure
Was unsurpassed in records of the mission.
Famine and pest had struck the Neutral tribes,
And fleeing squaws and children had invaded
The Petun villages for bread and refuge,
Inflicting on the cabins further pest
And further famine. When the priests arrived,

120

They found that their black cassocks had become
The symbols of the scourge. Children exclaimed –
"Disease and famine are outside." The women
Called to their young and fled to forest shelters,
Or hid them in the shadows of the cabins.
The men broke through a never-broken custom,
Denying the strangers right to food and rest.
Observing the two priests at prayer, the chief
Called out in *council voice* – *"What are these demons
Who take such unknown postures, what are they
But spells to make us die – to finish those
Disease had failed to kill inside our cabins?"*
Driven from town to town with all doors barred,
Pursued by storms of threats and flying hatchets,
The priests sought refuge through the forest darkness
Back to the palisades of Sainte Marie.

As bleak an outlook faced Brébeuf when he
And Chaumonot took their November tramp –
Five forest days – to the north shores of Erie,
Where the most savage of the tribes – the Neutrals –
Packed their twelve thousand into forty towns.
Evil report had reached the settlements
By faster routes, for when upon the eve
Of the new mission Chaumonot had stated
The purpose of the journey, Huron chiefs,
Convinced by their own sorcerers that Brébeuf
Had laid the epidemic on the land,
Resolved to make the Neutral leaders agents
Of their revenge: for it was on Brébeuf,
The chieftain of the robes, that hate was centred.
They had the reason why the drums had failed
The hunt, why moose and deer had left the forest,
And why the Manitou who sends the sun
And rain upon the corn, lures to the trap
The beaver, trains the arrow on the goose,
Had not responded to the chants and cries.
The magic of the "breathings" had not cured
The sick and dying. Was it not the prayers

To the new God which cast malignant spells?
The rosary against the amulet?
The Blackrobes with that water-rite performed
Upon the children – with that new sign
Of wood or iron held up before the eyes
Of the stricken? Did the Indian not behold
Death following hard upon the offered Host?
Was not *Echon* Brébeuf the evil one?
Still, all attempts to kill him were forestalled,
For awe and fear had mitigated fury:
His massive stature, courage never questioned,
His steady glance, the firmness of his voice,
And that strange nimbus of authority,
In some dim way related to their gods,
Had kept the bowstrings of the Hurons taut
At the arrow feathers, and the javelin poised
And hesitant. But now cunning might do
What fear forbade. A brace of Huron runners
Were sped to the Neutral country with rich bribes
To put the priests to death. And so Brébeuf
And his companion entered the first town
With famine in their cheeks only to find
Worse than the Petun greetings – corn refused,
Whispers of death and screams of panic, flight
From incarnated plague, and while the chiefs
In closest council on the Huron terms
Voted for life or death, the younger men
Outside drew nearer to the priests, cursed them,
Spat at them while convulsive hands were clutching
At hatchet helves, waiting impatiently
The issue of that strident rhetoric
Shaking the cabin bark. The council ended,
The feeling strong for death but ruled by fears,
For if those foreign spirits had the power
To spread the blight upon the land, what could
Their further vengeance not exact? Besides,
What lay behind those regimental colours
And those new drums reported from Quebec?
The older men had qualified the sentence –

The priests at once must leave the Neutral land,
All cabins to be barred against admission,
No food, no shelter, and return immediate.
Defying threats, the Fathers spent four months,
Four winter months, besieging half the towns
In their pursuit of souls, for days their food
Boiled lichens, ground-nuts, star-grass bulbs and roots
Of the wild columbine. Met at the doors
By screams and blows, they would betake themselves
To the evergreens for shelter over-night.
And often, when the body strength was sapped
By the day's toil and there were streaks of blood
Inside the moccasins, when the last lodge
Rejected them as lepers and the welts
Hung on their shoulders, then the Fathers sought
The balm that never failed. Under the stars,
Along an incandescent avenue
The visions trembled, tender, placid, pure,
More beautiful than the doorway of Rheims
And sweeter than the Galilean fields.
For what was hunger and the burn of wounds
In those assuaging, healing moments when
The clearing mists revealed the face of Mary
And the lips of Jesus breathing benedictions?

At dawn they came back to the huts to get
The same rebuff of speech and club. A brave
Repulsed them at the palisade with axe
Uplifted – *"I have had enough,"* he said,
*"Of the dark flesh of my enemies. I mean
To kill and eat the white flesh of the priests."*
So close to death starvation and assault
Had led them and so meagre of result
Were all their ministrations that they thought
This was the finish of the enterprise.
The winter ended in futility.
And on their journey home the Fathers took
A final blow when March leagued with the natives
Unleashed a northern storm, piled up the snow-drifts,

Broke on the ice the shoulder of Brébeuf,
And stumbled them for weeks before she sent
Them limping through the postern of the fort.
Upon his bed that night Brébeuf related
A vision he had seen – a moving cross,
Its upright beam arising from the south –
The country of the Iroquois: the shape
Advanced along the sky until its arms
Cast shadows on the Huron territory,
"And huge enough to crucify us all".

(THE STORY OF JOGUES)

VII
Bad days had fallen on Huronia.
A blight of harvest, followed by a winter
In which unusual snowfall had thinned out
The hunting and reduced the settlements
To destitution, struck its hardest blow
At Sainte Marie. The last recourse in need,
The fort had been a common granary
And now the bins were empty. Altar-ware,
Vessels, linens, pictures lost or damaged;
Vestments were ragged, writing paper spent.
The Eucharist requiring bread and wine,
Quebec eight hundred miles away, a war
Freshly renewed – the Iroquois (Dutch-armed [38]
And seething with the memories of Champlain)
Arrayed against the French and Huron allies.

1642

The priests assessed the perils of the journey,
And the lot fell on Jogues to lead it. He,
Next to Brébeuf, had borne the heaviest brunt –
The Petun mission, then the following year,
The Ojibway where, after a hundred leagues,
Canoe and trail, accompanied by Raymbault,
He reached the shores of Lake Superior,
"And planted a great cross, facing it west".

The soundest of them all in legs, he gathered
A band of Huron traders and set out,
His task made double by the care of Raymbault
Whose health was broken mortally. He reached
Quebec with every day of the five weeks
A miracle of escape. A few days there,
With churches, hospitals, the Indian school
At Sillery, pageant and ritual,
Making their due impression on the minds
Of the Huron guides, Jogues with his band of forty
Packed the canoes and started back. Mohawks,
Enraged that on the east-bound trip the party
Had slipped their hands, awaited them, ambushed
Within the grass and reeds along the shore.

(THE ACCOUNT OF JOGUES' CAPTURE AND ENSLAVE-
MENT BY THE MOHAWKS AS TAKEN FROM HIS LETTER
TO HIS PROVINCIAL, JEAN FILLEAU, DATED AUGUST
5, 1643.)

"Unskilled in speech, in knowledge and not knowing
The precious hour of my visitation,
I beg you, if this letter chance to come
Unto your hands that in your charity
You aid me with your Holy Sacrifices
And with the earnest prayers of the whole Province,
As being among a people barbarous
In birth and manners, for I know that when
You will have heard this story you will see
The obligation under which I am
To God and my deep need of spiritual help.
Our business finished at Quebec, the feast
Of Saint Ignatius celebrated, we
Embarked for the Hurons. On the second day
Our men discovered on the shore fresh tracks
Thought by Eustache, experienced in war,
To be the footprints of our enemies.
A mile beyond we met them, twelve canoes
And seventy men. Abandoning the boats,
Most of the Hurons fled to a thick wood,
Leaving but twelve to put up the best front

125

We could, but seeing further Iroquois
Paddling so swiftly from the other shore,
We ceased from our defence and fled to cover
Of tree and bulrush. Watching from my shelter
The capture of Goupil and Indian converts,
I could not find it in my mind to leave them;
But as I was their comrade on the journey,
And should be made their comrade in the perils,
I gave myself as prisoner to the guard.
Likewise Eustache, always devoted, valiant,
Returned, exclaiming 'I praise God that He
Has granted me my prayer – that I should live
And die with you.' And then Guillaume Couture
Who, young and fleet, having outstripped his foe,
But finding flight intolerable came back
Of his free will, saying 'I cannot leave
My father in the hands of enemies.'
On him the Iroquois let loose their first
Assault for in the skirmish he had slain
A chief. They stripped him naked; with their teeth
They macerated his finger tips, tore off
The nails and pierced his right hand with a spear,
Couture taking the pain without a cry.
Then turning on Goupil and me they beat
Us to the ground under a flurry of fists
And knotted clubs, dragging us up half-dead
To agonize us with the finger torture.
And this was just the foretaste of our trials:
Dividing up as spoils of war our food,
Our clothes and books and vessels for the church,
They led or drove us on our six weeks' journey,
Our wounds festering under the summer sun.
At night we were the objects of their sport –
They mocked us by the plucking of our hair
From head and beard. And on the eighth day meeting
A band of warriors from the tribe on march
To attack the Richelieu fort, they celebrated
By disembarking all the captives, making
Us run the line beneath a rain of clubs.

And following that they placed us on the scaffolds,
Dancing around us hurling jests and insults.
Each one of us attempted to sustain
The other in his courage by no cry
Or sign of our infirmities. Eustache,
His thumbs wrenched off, withstood unconquerably
The probing of a stick which like a skewer
Beginning with the freshness of a wound
On the left hand was pushed up to the elbow.
And yet next day they put us on the route
Again — three days on foot and without food.
Through village after village we were led
In triumph with our backs shedding the skin
Under the sun — by day upon the scaffolds,
By night brought to the cabins where, cord-bound,
We lay on the bare earth while fiery coals
Were thrown upon our bodies. A long time
Indeed and cruelly have the wicked wrought
Upon my back with sticks and iron rods.
But though at times when left alone I wept,
Yet I thanked Him who always giveth strength
To the weary (I will glory in the things
Concerning my infirmity, being made
A spectacle to God and to the angels,
A sport and a contempt to the barbarians)
That I was thus permitted to console
And animate the French and Huron converts,
Placing before their minds the thought of Him
Who bore against Himself the contradiction
Of sinners. Weak through hanging by my wrists
Between two poles, my feet not touching ground,
I managed through His help to reach the stage,
And with the dew from leaves of Turkish corn
Two of the prisoners I baptized. I called
To them that in their torment they should fix
Their eyes on me as I bestowed the sign
Of the last absolution. With the spirit
Of Christ, Eustache then in the fire entreated
His Huron friends to let no thought of vengeance

Arising from this anguish at the stake
Injure the French hope for an Iroquois peace.
Onnonhoaraton, a youthful captive,
They killed — the one who seeing me prepared
For torture interposed, offering himself
A sacrifice for me who had in bonds
Begotten him for Christ. Couture was seized
And dragged off as a slave. René Goupil,
While placing on a child's forehead the sign
Of the Cross was murdered by a sorcerer,
And then, a rope tied to his neck, was dragged
Through the whole village and flung in the River."

(THE LATER ACCOUNT)

A family of the Wolf Clan having lost
A son in battle, Jogues as substitute
Was taken in, half-son, half-slave, his work
The drudgery of the village, bearing water,
Lighting the fires, and clad in tatters made
To join the winter hunt, bear heavy packs
On scarred and naked shoulders in the trade
Between the villages. His readiness
To execute his tasks, unmurmuring,
His courage when he plunged into a river
To save a woman and a child who stumbled
Crossing a bridge made by a fallen tree,
Had softened for a time his master's harshness.
It gained him scattered hours of leisure when
He set his mind to work upon the language
To make concrete the articles of Faith.
At intervals he stole into the woods
To pray and meditate and carve the Name
Upon the bark. Out of the Mohawk spoils
At the first battle he had found and hid
Two books – *The Following of Christ* and one
Of Paul's *Epistles*, and with these when *"weary*
Even of life and pressed beyond all measure
Above his strength" he followed the *"running waters"*
To quench his thirst. But often would the hate

128

Of the Mohawk foes flame out anew when Jogues
Was on his knees muttering the magic words,
And when a hunting party empty-handed
Returned or some reverse was met in battle,
Here was the victim ready at their door.
Believing that a band of warriors
Had been destroyed, they seized the priest and set
His day of death, but at the eleventh hour,
With the arrival of a group of captives,
The larger festival of torture gave
Him momentary reprieve. Yet when he saw
The holocaust and rushed into the flames
To save a child, a heavy weight laid hold
Upon his spirit lasting many days –
"My life wasted with grief, my years with sighs;
Oh wherefore was I born that I should see
The ruin of my people! Woe is me!
But by His favour I shall overcome
Until my change is made and He appear."

This story of enslavement had been brought
To Montmagny, the Governor of Quebec,
And to the outpost of the Dutch, Fort Orange.
Quebec was far away and, short of men,
Could never cope with the massed Iroquois,
Besides, Jogues' letter begged the Governor
That no measures *"to save a single life"*
Should hurt the cause of France. To the Provincial
He wrote – *"Who in my absence would console*
The captives? Who absolve the penitent?
Encourage them in torments? Who baptize
The dying? On this cross to which our Lord
Has nailed me with Himself am I resolved
To live and die."
                          And when the commandant
Of the Dutch fort sent notice that a ship
At anchor in the Hudson would provide
Asylum, Jogues delayed that he might seek
Counsel of God and satisfy his conscience,

129

Lest some intruding self-preserving thought
Conflict with duty. Death was certain soon.
He knew it – for that mounting tide of hate
Could not be checked: it had engulfed his friends;
'Twould take him next. How close to suicide
Would be refusal? Not as if escape
Meant dereliction: no, his early vows
Were still inviolate – he would return.
He pledged himself to God there on his knees
Before two bark-strips fashioned as a cross
Under the forest trees – his oratory.
And so, one night, the Indians asleep,
Jogues left the house, fumbling his darkened way,
Half-walk, half-crawl, a lacerated leg
Making the journey of one-half a mile
The toil of half a night. By dawn he found
The shore, and, single-handed, pushed a boat,
Stranded by ebb-tide, down the slope of sand
To the river's edge and rowed out to the ship,
Where he was lifted up the side by sailors
Who, fearful of the risk of harbouring
A fugitive, carried him to the hatch
And hid him with the cargo in the hold.
The outcry in the morning could be heard
Aboard the ship as Indians combed the cabins,
Threatened the guards and scoured the neighbouring
    woods,
And then with strong suspicion of the vessel
Demanded of the officers their captive.
After two days Jogues with his own consent
Was taken to the fort and hid again
Behind the barrels of a store. For weeks
He saw and heard the Mohawks as they passed,
Examining cordage, prying into casks,
At times touching his clothes, but missing him
As he lay crouched in darkness motionless.
With evidence that he was in the fort,
The Dutch abetting the escape, the chiefs
Approached the commandant – *"The prisoner*

Is ours. He is not of your race or speech.
The Dutch are friends: the Frenchmen are our foes.
Deliver up this priest into our hands."
The cries were countered by the officer —
"He is like us in blood if not in tongue.
The Frenchman here is under our protection.
He is our guest. We treat him as you treat
The strangers in your cabins, for you feed
And shelter them. That also is our law,
The custom of our nation." Argument
Of no avail, a ransom price was offered,
Refused, but running up the bargain scale,
It caught the Mohawks at three hundred livres,
And Jogues at last was safely on the Hudson.

The tale of Jogues' first mission to the Hurons
Ends on a sequel briefly sung but keyed
To the tune of the story, for the stretch
Home was across a wilderness, his bed
A coil of rope on a ship's open deck
Swept by December surge. The voyage closed
At Falmouth where, robbed by a pirate gang,
He wandered destitute until picked up
By a French crew who offered him tramp fare.
He landed on the shore of Brittany
On Christmas Eve, and by New Year he reached
The Jesuit establishment at Rennes.

The trumpets blew once more, and Jogues returned
With the spring expedition to Quebec.
Honoured by Montmagny, he took the post
Of peace ambassador to hostile tribes,
And then the orders came from Lalemant
That he should open up again the cause
Among the Mohawks at Ossernenon.   40
Jogues knew that he was travelling to his death,
And though each hour of that former mission
Burned at his finger stumps, the wayward flesh
Obeyed the summons. Lalemant as well
Had known the peril — had he not re-named

131

Ossernenon, the Mission of the Martyrs?
So Jogues, accompanied by his friend Lalande
Departed for the village – his last letter
To his Superior read: *"I will return*
Cost it a thousand lives. I know full well
That I shall not survive, but He who helped
Me by His grace before will never fail me
Now when I go to do His holy will."
And to the final consonant the vow
Was kept, for two days after they had struck
The town, their heads were on the palisades,
And their dragged bodies flung into the Mohawk.

1646

(BRESSANI)

VIII

The western missions waiting Jogues' return
Were held together by a scarlet thread.
The forays of the Iroquois had sent
The fugitive survivors to the fort.
Three years had passed – and where was Jogues? The
    scant
Supplies of sagamite could never feed
The inflow from the stricken villages.
The sparse reports had filtered to Quebec
And the command was given to Bressani
To lead the rescue band to Sainte Marie.
Leaving Three Rivers in the spring when ice
Was on the current, he was caught like Jogues,
With his six Hurons and a French oblate,
A boy of twelve; transferred to Iroquois'
Canoes and carried up the Richelieu;
Disbarked and driven through the forest trails
To Lake Champlain; across it; and from there
Around the rocks and marshes to the Hudson.
And every time a camp was built and fires
Were laid the torment was renewed; in all
The towns the squaws and children were regaled

With evening festivals upon the scaffolds.
Bressani wrote one day when vigilance
Relaxed and his split hand was partly healed —
"I do not know if your Paternity
Will recognize this writing for the letter
Is soiled. Only one finger of the hand
Is left unburned. The blood has stained the paper.
My writing table is the earth; the ink
Gunpowder mixed with water." And again —
This time to his Superior — *"I could*
Not have believed it to be possible
That a man's body was so hard to kill."
The earlier fate of Jogues was his — enslaved,
But ransomed at Fort Orange by the Dutch;
Restored to partial health; sent to Rochelle
In the autumn, but in April back again
And under orders for the Huron mission,
Where he arrived this time unscathed to take
A loyal welcome from his priestly comrades.

Bressani's presence stimulated faith
Within the souls of priests and neophytes.
The stories burned like fuel of the faggots —
Jogues' capture and his rock stability,
And the no less triumphant stand Eustache
Had made showing the world that native metal
Could take the test as nobly as the French.
And Ragueneau's letter to his General stated —
"Bressani ill-equipped to speak the Huron
Has speech more eloquent to capture souls:
It is his scars, his mutilated hands.
'Only show us,' the neophytes exclaim,
'The wounds, for they teach better than our tongues
Your faith, for you have come again to face
The dangers. Only thus we know that you
Believe the truth and would have us believe it.' "

IX
In those three years since Jogues' departure doubts
Though unexpressed had visited the mission.

133

For death had come to several in the fold –
Raymbault, Goupil, Eustache, and worse than death
To Jogues, and winter nights were bleaker, darker
Without the company of Brébeuf. Lion
Of limb and heart, he had entrenched the faith,
Was like a triple palisade himself.
But as his broken shoulder had not healed,
And ordered to Quebec by Lalemant,
He took the leave that seven years of work
Deserved. The city hailed him with delight.
For more than any other did he seem
The very incarnation of the age –
Champlain the symbol of exploring France,
Tracking the rivers to their lairs, Brébeuf
The token of a nobler chivalry.
He went the rounds of the stations, saw the gains
The East had made in converts – Sillery
For Indians and Notre Dame des Anges
For the French colonists; convents and schools
Flourished. Why should the West not have the same
Yield for the sowing? It was labourers
They needed with supplies and adequate
Defence. St. Lawrence and the Ottawa
Infested by the Iroquois were traps
Of death. Three bands of Hurons had been caught
That summer. Montmagny had warned the priest
Against the risk of unprotected journeys.
So when the reinforcements came from France,
Brébeuf set out under a guard of soldiers
Taking with him two young recruits – Garreau
And Chabanel – arriving at the fort
In the late fall. The soldiers wintered there
And supervised defensive strategy.
Replaced the forlorn feelings with fresh hopes,
And for two years the mission enterprise
Renewed its lease of life. Rumours of treaties
Between the French and Mohawks stirred belief
That peace was in the air, that other tribes
Inside the Iroquois Confederacy

41

134

Might enter – with the Hurons sharing terms.
This was the pipe-dream – was it credible?
The ranks of missionaries were filling up:
At Sainte Marie, Brébeuf and Ragueneau,
Le Mercier, Chastellain and Chabanel;
St. Joseph – Garnier and René Menard;
St. Michel – Chaumonot and Du Peron;
The others – Claude Pijart, Le Moyne, Garreau
And Daniel
                    What validity the dream
Possessed was given by the seasonal
Uninterrupted visits of the priests
To their loved home, both fort and residence.
Here they discussed their plans, and added up
In smiling rivalry their tolls of converts:
They loitered at the shelves, fondled the books,
Running their fingers down the mellowed pages
As if they were the faces of their friends.
They stood for hours before the saints or knelt
Before the Virgin and the crucifix
In mute transfiguration. These were hours
That put the bandages upon their hurts,
Making their spirits proof against all ills
That had assailed or could assail the flesh,
Turned winter into spring and made return
To their far mission posts an exaltation.
The bell each morning called the neophytes
To Mass, again at evening, and the tones
Lured back the memories across the seas.
And often in the summer hours of twilight
When Norman chimes were ringing, would the priests
Forsake the fort and wander to the shore
To sing the *Gloria* while hermit thrushes
Rivalled the rapture of the nightingales.

The native register was rich in name
And number. Earlier years had shown results
Mainly among the young and sick and aged,
Where little proof was given of the root

Of faith, but now the Fathers told of deeds
That flowered from the stems. Had not Eustache
Bequeathed his record like a Testament?
The sturdiest warriors and chiefs had vied
Among themselves within the martyr ranks: —
Stories of captives led to sacrifice,
Accepting scaffold fires under the rites,
Enduring to the end, had taken grip
Of towns and clans. St. Joseph had its record
For Garnier reported that Totiri,
A native of high rank, while visiting
St. Ignace when a torture was in progress,
Had emulated Jogues by plunging through
The flaming torches that he might apply
The Holy Water to an Iroquois.
Garreau and Pijart added lists of names
From the Algonquins and the Nipissings,
And others told of Pentecostal meetings
In cabins by the Manitoulin shores.

Not only was the faith sustained by hopes
Nourished within the bosom of their home
And by the wish-engendered talk of peace,
But there outside the fort was evidence
Of tenure for the future. Acres rich
In soil extended to the forest fringe.
Each year they felled the trees and burned the stumps,
Pushing the frontier back, clearing the land,
Spading, hoeing. The stomach's noisy protest
At sagamite and wild rice found a rest
With bread from wheat, fresh cabbages and pease,
And squashes which when roasted had the taste
Of Norman apples. Strawberries in July,
October beechnuts, pepper roots for spice,
And at the bottom of a spring that flowed
Into a pond shaded by silver birches
And ringed by marigolds was water-cress
In chilled abundance. So, was this the West?
The Wilderness? That flight of tanagers;

Those linguals from the bobolinks; those beeches,
Roses and water-lilies; at the pools
Those bottle-gentians! For a time the fields
Could hypnotize the mind to scenes of France.
Within five years the change was wrought. The cocks
Were crowing in the yards, and in the pasture
Were sheep and cows and pigs that had been brought
As sucklings that immense eight hundred miles
In sacks – canoed, and portaged on the shoulders.
The traders, like the soldiers, too, had heard
Of a great ocean larger than the Huron.
Was it the western gateway to Cathay?
The Passage? Master-theme of song and ballad;   42
The *myth* at last resolved into the *fact*!
Along that route, it was believed, French craft
Freighted with jewels, spices, tapestries,
Would sail to swell the coffers of the Bourbons.   43
Such was the dream though only buffalo roamed
The West and autumn slept upon the prairies.

This dream was at its brightest now, Quebec
Was building up a western citadel
In Sainte Marie. With sixty Frenchmen there,
The eastern capital itself had known
Years less auspicious. Might the fort not be
The bastion to one-half the continent,
New France expanding till the longitudes
Staggered the daring of the navigators?
The priests were breathless with another space
Beyond the measure of the astrolabe –
A different empire built upon the pulses,
Where even the sun and moon and stars revolved
Around a Life and a redemptive Death.
They pushed their missions to the north and west
Further into Algonquin territories,
Among the Ottawas at Manitoulin,
And towards the Ojibways at Sault Sainte Marie.
New village groups were organized in stations –
St. Magdalen, St. Jean, and St. Matthias.

Had Chabanel, ecstatic with success,
Not named one fort the Village of Believers?
Brébeuf was writing to his General —
"Peace, union and tranquillity are here
Between the members of our Order. We need
More workers for the apostolic field,
Which more than ever whitens for the harvest."
And to this call came Gabriel Lalemant,
Bonin, Daran, Greslon, besides a score
Of labourers and soldiers. In one year
Twelve hundred converts, churches over-crowded,
With Mass conducted in the open air!

And so the seasons passed. When the wild ducks
Forsook the Huron marshes for the south,
It was the signal for the priests to pack
Their blankets. Not until the juncos came,
And flickers tapped the crevices of bark,
And the bloodroot was pushing through the leaf-mould,
Would they reset their faces towards their home.

X

While Ragueneau's *Relations* were being sent
Homeward, picturing the promise of the west,
The thunder clouds were massing in the east
Under the pounding drums. The treaty signed
Between the Iroquois and Montmagny
Was broken by the murder of Lalande
And Jogues. The news had drifted to the fort —
The prelude only to the heavier blows
And deeper treachery. The Iroquois,
Infesting lake and stream, forest and shore,
Were trapping soldiers, traders, Huron guides:
The whole confederacy was on the march.
Both waterways were blocked, the quicker route —
St. Lawrence, and the arduous Ottawa.
They caught the Hurons at their camps, surprised
Canoe-fleets from the reeds and river bends
And robbed them, killed them on the portages.
So widespread were their forays, they encountered

Bands of Algonquins on the hunt, slew them,
Dispersed them from their villages and sent
Survivors to the northern wilderness.
So keen their lust for slaughter, they enticed
The Huron chieftains under pledge of truce
And closed negotiations with their scalps.

As the months passed the pressure of attack
Moved grimly towards the west, making complete
The isolation of Huronia.
No commerce with Quebec – no traveller
For a whole year came to the Residence.
But constant was the stream of fugitives
From smaller undefended villages,
Fleeing west and ever west. The larger towns,
The deluge breaking down their walls, drove on
The surplus to their neighbours which, in turn,
Urged on the panic herd to Sainte Marie.
This mother of the missions felt the strain
As one by one the buffers were destroyed,
And the flocks came nearer for their pasturage.
There could be only one conclusion when
The priests saw the migration of the missions –
That of St. Jean four times abandoning
Its stations and four times establishing
New centres with a more improved defence;
That of St. Ignace where a double raid
That slaughtered hundreds, lifted bodily
Both town and mission, driving to their last
Refuge the ragged remnants. Yet Ragueneau
Was writing – *"We are here as yet intact
But all determined to shed blood and life
If need be. In this Residence still reigns
The peace and love of Heaven. Here the sick
Will find a hospital, the travellers
A place of rest, the fugitives, asylum.
During the year more than three thousand persons
Have sought and found shelter under our roof.
We have dispensed the Bread of Life to all*

And we have fed their bodies, though our fare
Is down to one food only, crushed corn boiled
And seasoned with the powder of smoked fish."

Despite the perils, Sainte Marie was sending
Her missionaries afield, revisiting
The older sites, establishing the new,
With that same measure of success and failure
Which tested courage or confirmed a faith.
Garreau, sick and expecting death, was brought
By Pijart and a French assistant back
From the Algonquin wastes, for thirteen days
Borne by a canoe and by his comrades' shoulders.
Recovering even after the last rites
Had been administered, he faced the task
Again. Fresh visits to the Petun tribes
Had little yield but cold and starving days,
Unsheltered nights, the same fare at the doors,
Savoured by Jogues and Garnier seven years
Before. And everywhere the labourers worked
Under a double threat – the Iroquois,
And the Huron curse inspired by sorcerers
Who saw black magic in the Jesuit robes
And linked disaster with their ritual.
Between the hammer and the anvil now
Huronia was laid and the first priest
To take the blow was Daniel.

                              Fourteen years
This priest had laboured at the Huron mission.
Following a week of rest at Sainte Marie
He had returned to his last post, St. Joseph,
Where he had built his church and for the year
Just gone had added to his charge the hundreds
Swarming from villages stormed by the foe.
And now in that inexorable order,
Station by station, town by town, it was
St. Joseph's turn. Aware that the main force
Of Huron warriors had left the town,
The Iroquois had breached the palisade

And, overwhelming the defenders, sacked
And burned the cabins. Mass had just been offered,
When the war yells were heard and Daniel came
Outside. Seeing the panic, fully knowing
Extinction faced the town with this invasion,
And that ten precious minutes of delay
Might give his flock the refuge of the woods,
He faced the vanguard of the Iroquois,
And walked with firm selective dignity
As in the manner of a parley. Fear
And wonder checked the Indians at the sight
Of a single dark-robed, unarmed challenger
Against arrows, muskets, spears and tomahawks.
That momentary pause had saved the lives
Of hundreds as they fled into the forest,
But not the life of Daniel. Though afraid
At first to cross a charmed circumference
To take a struggle hand-to-hand, they drove
Their arrows through him, then in frenzied rush
Mastering their awe, they hurled themselves upon
The body, stripped it of its clothes and flung it
Into the burning church. By noon nothing
Remained but ashes of the town, the fort,
The cabins and their seven hundred dead.

July, 1648

XI

Ragueneau was distraught. He was shepherd-priest.
Daniel was first to die under his care,
And nigh a score of missionaries were lost
In unprotected towns. Besides, he knew
He could not, if he would, resist that mob
That clamoured at the stockades, day by day.
His moral supervision was bound up
With charity that fed and warmed and healed.
And through the winter following Daniel's death
Six thousand Indians sought shelter there.
The season's crops to the last grain were garnered
And shared. *"Through the kind Providence of God,*

We managed, as it were, to draw both oil
And honey from the very stones around us.
The obedience, patience of our missionaries
Excel reward — all with one heart and soul
Infused with the high spirit of our Order;
The servants, boys, and soldiers day and night
Working beyond their strength! Here is the service
Of joy, that we will take whatever God
Ordains for us whether it be life or death."
The challenge was accepted, for the spring
Opened upon the hardest tragic blows
The iron in the human soul could stand.

St. Louis and St. Ignace still remained
The flying buttresses of Sainte Marie.
From them the Residence received reports
Daily of movements of the Iroquois.
Much labour had been spent on their defence.
Ramparts of pine fifteen feet high enclosed
St. Louis. On three sides a steep ravine
Topped by the stakes made nigh impregnable
St. Ignace; then the palisaded fourth,
Subject alone to a surprise assault,
Could rally the main body of defenders.
The Iroquois, alert as eagles, knew
The weakness of the Hurons, the effect
On the morale of unexpected raids
Committing towns to fire and pushing back
The eastern ramparts. Piece by piece, the rim
Was being cracked and fissures driven down
The bowl: and stroke by stroke the strategy
Pointed to Sainte Marie. Were once the fort
Now garrisoned by forty Frenchmen taken,
No power predicted from Quebec could save
The Huron nation from its doom. St. Ignace
Lay in the path but during the eight months
After St. Joseph's fall the enemy
Had leisurely prepared their plans. Their scouts
Reported that one-half of the town's strength

Was lost by flight and that an apathy,
In spite of all the priests could do to stem it,
Had seized the invaded tribes. They knew that when
The warriors were hunting in the forest
This weaker palisade was scalable.
And the day came in March when the whole fate
That overtook St. Joseph in July
Swept on St. Ignace – sudden and complete.
The Mohawks and the Senecas uniting,
A thousand strong, the town bereft of fighters,
Four hundred old and young inside the stakes,
The assault was made two hours before the dawn.
But half-aroused from sleep, many were killed
Within their cabins. Of the four hundred three
Alone managed to reach the woods to scream
The alarm to the drowsed village of St. Louis.

At nine o'clock that morning – such the speed
Of the pursuit – a guard upon the hill
Behind the Residence was watching whiffs
Of smoke to the south, but a league away.
Bush fires? Not with this season's depth of snow.
The Huron bivouacs? The settlements
Too close for that. Camps of the Iroquois?
Not while cunning and stealth controlled their tactics.
The smoke was in the town. The morning air,
Clearing, could leave no doubt of that, and just
As little that the darkening pall could spring
Out of the vent-holes from the cabin roofs.
Ragueneau rushed to the hill at the guard's call;
Summoned Bressani; sheets and tongues of flame
Leaping some fifty feet above the smoke
Meant to their eyes the capture and the torch –
St. Louis with Brébeuf and Lalemant!

Less than two hours it took the Iroquois
To capture, sack and garrison St. Ignace,
And start then for St. Louis. The alarm
Sounded, five hundred of the natives fled
To the mother fort only to be pursued

143

And massacred in the snow. The eighty braves
That manned the stockades perished at the breaches;
And what was seen by Ragueneau and the guard
Was smoke from the massed fire of cabin bark.

Brébeuf and Lalemant were not numbered
In the five hundred of the fugitives.
They had remained, infusing nerve and will
In the defenders, rushing through the cabins
Baptizing and absolving those who were
Too old, too young, too sick to join the flight.
And when, resistance crushed, the Iroquois
Took all they had not slain back to St. Ignace,
The vanguard of the prisoners were the priests.

March 16, 1649

Three miles from town to town over the snow,
Naked, laden with pillage from the lodges,
The captives filed like wounded beasts of burden,
Three hours on the march, and those that fell
Or slowed their steps were killed.

                      Three days before
Brébeuf had celebrated his last mass.
And he had known it was to be the last.
There was prophetic meaning as he took
The cord and tied the alb around his waist,
Attached the maniple to his left arm
And drew the seamless purple chasuble
With the large cross over his head and shoulders,
Draping his body: every vestment held
An immediate holy symbol as he whispered –
"Upon my head the helmet of Salvation.
So purify my heart and make me white;
With this cincture of purity gird me,
O Lord.
           May I deserve this maniple
Of sorrow and of penance.
                  Unto me
Restore the stole of immortality.

My yoke is sweet, my burden light.
                                  Grant that
I may so bear it as to win Thy grace."

Entering, he knelt before as rude an altar
As ever was reared within a sanctuary,
But hallowed as that chancel where the notes
Of Palestrina's score had often pealed
The *Assumpta est Maria* through Saint Peter's.
For, covered in the centre of the table,
Recessed and sealed, a hollowed stone contained
A relic of a charred or broken body
Which perhaps a thousand years ago or more
Was offered as a sacrifice to Him
Whose crucifix stood there between the candles.
And on the morrow would this prayer be answered: —
"Eternal Father, I unite myself
With the affections and the purposes
Of Our Lady of Sorrows on Calvary.
And now I offer Thee the sacrifice
Which Thy Beloved Son made of Himself
Upon the Cross and now renews on this,
His holy altar . . .
                    Graciously receive
My life for His life as he gave His life
For mine . . .
              This is my body.
                                In like manner . . .
Take ye and drink — the chalice of my blood."

XII

No doubt in the mind of Brébeuf that this was the last
Journey — three miles over the snow. He knew
That the margins as thin as they were by which he escaped
From death through the eighteen years of his mission toil
Did not belong to this chapter: not by his pen
Would this be told. He knew his place in the line,
For the blaze of the trail that was cut on the bark by
    Jogues
Shone still. He had heard the story as told by writ

And word of survivors – of how a captive slave
Of the hunters, the skin of his thighs cracked with the
    frost,
He would steal from the tents to the birches, make a
    rough cross
From two branches, set it in snow and on the peel
Inscribe his vows and dedicate to the Name
In "litanies of love" what fragments were left
From the wrack of his flesh; of his escape from the tribes;
Of his journey to France where he knocked at the door
    of the College
Of Rennes, was gathered in as a mendicant friar,
Nameless, unknown, till he gave for proof to the priest
His scarred credentials of faith, the nail-less hands
And withered arms – the signs of the Mohawk fury.
Nor yet was the story finished – he had come again
Back to his mission to get the second death.
And the comrades of Jogues – Goupil, Eustache and
    Couture,
Had been stripped and made to run the double files
And take the blows – one hundred clubs to each line –
And this as the prelude to torture, leisured, minute,
Where thorns on the quick, scallop shells to the joints
    of the thumbs,
Provided the sport for children and squaws till the end.
And adding salt to the blood of Brébeuf was the thought
Of Daniel – was it months or a week ago?
So far, so near, it seemed in time, so close
In leagues – just over there to the south it was
He faced the arrows and died in front of his church.

But winding into the greater artery
Of thought that bore upon the coming passion
Were little tributaries of wayward wish
And reminiscence. Paris with its vespers
Was folded in the mind of Lalemant,
And the soft Gothic lights and traceries
Were shading down the ridges of his vows.
But two years past at Bourges he had walked the cloisters,

146

Companioned by Saint Augustine and Francis,
And wrapped in quiet holy mists. Brébeuf,
His mind a moment throwing back the curtain
Of eighteen years, could see the orchard lands,
The *cidreries*, the peasants at the Fairs,
The undulating miles of wheat and barley,
Gardens and pastures rolling like a sea
From Lisieux to Le Havre. Just now the surf
Was pounding on the limestone Norman beaches
And on the reefs of Calvados. Had dawn   45
This very day not flung her surplices
Around the headlands and with golden fire
Consumed the silken argosies that made
For Rouen from the estuary of the Seine?
A moment only for that veil to lift –
A moment only for those bells to die
That rang their matins at Condé-sur-Vire.   46

By noon St. Ignace! The arrival there
The signal for the battle-cries of triumph,
The gauntlet of the clubs. The stakes were set
And the ordeal of Jogues was re-enacted
Upon the priests – even with wilder fury,
For here at last was trapped their greatest victim,
Echon. The Iroquois had waited long
For this event. Their hatred for the Hurons
Fused with their hatred for the French and priests
Was to be vented on this sacrifice,
And to that camp had come apostate Hurons,
United with their foes in common hate
To settle up their reckoning with *Echon*.

*   *   *   *   *

Now three o'clock, and capping the height of the passion,
Confusing the sacraments under the pines of the forest,
Under the incense of balsam, under the smoke
Of the pitch, was offered the rite of the font. On the head,
The breast, the loins and the legs, the boiling water!
While the mocking paraphrase of the symbols was hurled

147

At their faces like shards of flint from the arrow heads –
"We baptize thee with water . . .

> *That thou mayest be led*

To Heaven . . .

> *To that end we do anoint thee.*

We treat thee as a friend: we are the cause
Of thy happiness; we are thy priests; the more
Thou sufferest, the more thy God will reward thee,
So give us thanks for our kind offices."

The fury of taunt was followed by fury of blow.
Why did not the flesh of Brébeuf cringe to the scourge,
Respond to the heat, for rarely the Iroquois found
A victim that would not cry out in such pain – yet here
The fire was on the wrong fuel. Whenever he spoke,
It was to rally the soul of his friend whose turn
Was to come through the night while the eyes were
    uplifted in prayer,
Imploring the Lady of Sorrows, the mother of Christ,
As pain brimmed over the cup and the will was called
To stand the test of the coals. And sometimes the speech
Of Brébeuf struck out, thundering reproof to his foes,
Half-rebuke, half-defiance, giving them roar for roar.
Was it because the chancel became the arena,
Brébeuf a lion at bay, not a lamb on the altar,
As if the might of a Roman were joined to the cause
Of Judaea? Speech they could stop for they girdled his
    lips,
But never a moan could they get. Where was the source
Of his strength, the home of his courage that topped the
    best
Of their braves and even out-fabled the lore of their
    legends?
In the bunch of his shoulders which often had carried a
    load
Extorting the envy of guides at an Ottawa portage?
The heat of the hatchets was finding a path to that source.
In the thews of his thighs which had mastered the trails
    of the Neutrals?

148

They would gash and beribbon those muscles. Was it
    the blood?
They would draw it fresh from its fountain. Was it the
    heart?
They dug for it, fought for the scraps in the way of the
    wolves.
But not in these was the valour or stamina lodged;
Nor in the symbol of Richelieu's robes or the seals
Of Mazarin's charters, nor in the stir of the *lilies*
Upon the Imperial folds; nor yet in the words
Loyola wrote on a table of lava-stone
In the cave of Manresa – not in these the source –   47
But in the sound of invisible trumpets blowing
Around two slabs of board, right-angled, hammered
By Roman nails and hung on a Jewish hill.

The wheel had come full circle with the visions
In France of Brébeuf poured through the mould of
    St. Ignace.
Lalemant died in the morning at nine, in the flame
Of the pitch belts. Flushed with the sight of the bodies,
    the foes
Gathered their clans and moved back to the north and
    west
To join in the fight against the tribes of the Petuns.
There was nothing now that could stem the Iroquois blast.
However undaunted the souls of the priests who were left,
However fierce the sporadic counter attacks
Of the Hurons striking in roving bands from the ambush,
Or smashing out at their foes in garrison raids,
The villages fell before a blizzard of axes
And arrows and spears, and then were put to the torch.

The days were dark at the fort and heavier grew
The burdens on Ragueneau's shoulders. Decision was his.
No word from the east could arrive in time to shape
The step he must take. To and fro – from altar to hill,
From hill to altar, he walked and prayed and watched.
As governing priest of the Mission he felt the pride
Of his Order whipping his pulse, for was not St. Ignace

The highest test of the Faith? And all that torture
And death could do to the body was done. The Will
And the Cause in their triumph survived.
Loyola's mountains,
Sublime at their summits, were scaled to the uttermost
    peak.
Ragueneau, the Shepherd, now looked on a battered fold.
In a whirlwind of fire St. Jean, like St. Joseph, crashed
Under the Iroquois impact. Firm at his post,
Garnier suffered the fate of Daniel. And now
Chabanel, last in the roll of the martyrs, entrapped
On his knees in the woods met death at apostate hands.

The drama was drawing close to its end. It fell
To Ragueneau's lot to perform a final rite –
To offer the fort in sacrificial fire!
He applied the torch himself. *"Inside an hour,"*
He wrote, *"we saw the fruit of ten years' labour*
Ascend in smoke, – then looked our last at the fields,
Put altar-vessels and food on a raft of logs,
And made our way to the island of St. Joseph."
But even from there was the old tale retold –
Of hunger and the search for roots and acorns;
Of cold and persecution unto death
By the Iroquois; of Jesuit will and courage
As the shepherd-priest with Chaumoñot led back
The remnant of a nation to Quebec.

THE MARTYRS' SHRINE

Three hundred years have passed, and the winds of God
Which blew over France are blowing once more through
    the pines
That bulwark the shores of the great Fresh Water Sea.
Over the wastes abandoned by human tread,
Where only the bittern's cry was heard at dusk;
Over the lakes where the wild ducks built their nests,
The skies that had banked their fires are shining again
With the stars that guided the feet of Jogues and Brébeuf.
The years as they turned have ripened the martyrs' seed,

And the ashes of St. Ignace are glowing afresh.
The trails, having frayed the threads of the cassocks, sank
Under the mould of the centuries, under fern
And brier and fungus – there in due time to blossom
Into the highways that lead to the crest of the hill
Which havened both shepherd and flock in the days of
   their trial.
For out of the torch of Ragueneau's ruins the candles
Are burning today in the chancel of Sainte Marie.
The Mission sites have returned to the fold of the Order.
Near to the ground where the cross broke under the
   hatchet,
And went with it into the soil to come back at the turn
Of the spade with the carbon and calcium char of the
   bodies,
The shrines and altars are built anew; the *Aves*
And prayers ascend, and the Holy Bread is broken.

Behind the Log

There is a language in a naval log
That rams the grammar down a layman's throat,
Where words unreel in paragraphs, and lines
In chapters. Volumes lie in graphs and codes,
Recording with an algebraic care
The idiom of storms, their lairs and paths;
Or, in the self-same bloodless manner, sorting
The mongrel litters of a battle signal
In victories or defeats or bare survivals,
Flags at half-mast, salutes and guards of honour,
Distinguished crosses, burials at sea.

Our navigators trained their astrolabes
And sextants on the skies in lucky weather,
Or added guesses to dead reckoning,
Hauled up their lead, examined mud or shell
Or gravel on the arming – fifty fathoms,
Now forty, thirty, twenty-five, shallowing
Quickly! *"Engines astern, reefs, keep your lead
Going. Have plenty of water under you."*
They did not wait till miracles of science
Unstopped the naked ears for supersonics,
Or lifted cataracts from finite vision
To make night and its darkness visible.
How long ago was it since sailors blew
Their sirens at the cliffs while nearing land,
Traversing channels, cocked their ears and waited?
"Where did you hear that echo, mate?"

                                    *"Right off
The starboard quarter, Captain. Took ten seconds."*
"That's Gull Rock there a mile away. Where now?"
"Two seconds for the echo from port bow."
"That's Porpoise Head I reckon – Hard a-port!"
With echoes everywhere, stand out to sea.
But when the winds deafened their ears or cloud
And rain blinded their eyes, they were shoved back
Upon their mother wit which either had

To find the exits to the runs and round
The Capes or pile their ships upon the reefs.

And of that lineage are the men today.
They still are calling to the rocks: they get
Their answers in the same hard terms: they call
To steel gliding beneath the sea: they pierce
Horizons for the surface hulls: they ping
The sky for the plane's fuselage: even
The moon acknowledged from her crater sills.
But though the radio bursts and vacuum tubes
And electronic beams were miracles
Of yesterday, dismissing cloud and rain
And darkness as illusions of the sense,
Yet always there to watch the colours, note
The V-break in the beam's straight line, to hear
The echoes, feel the pain, are eyes, ears, nerves:
Always remains the guess within the judgment
To jump the fine perfection of the physics
And smell mortality behind the log.

As weird a game of ping-pong ever played
Was on the sea – the place, off Cape Farewell,
With the back-curtain of the Greenland ice-cap:
Time – '41 autumnal equinox.
The crisis was the imminence of famine
And the cutting of the ganglia and veins
That vitalized the sinews, fed the cells
Of lungs demanding oxygen in air.
The wicks were guttering from want of oil,
And without oil, the bread went with the light,
And without bread, the will could not sustain
The fight, piping its courage to the heart.

Grey predatory fish had pedigreed
With tiger sharks and brought a speed and power
The sharks had never known, for they had been
Committed to the sea under a charter
Born of a mania of mind and will
And nurtured by a Messianic slogan.

They were not bounded by the parallels.
They found their habitats wherever there
Was open sea and keels to ride upon it.
Off the North Cape they had outsped the narwhals,
The sawfish off the Rios and the Horn.
They did not kill for food: they killed that food
Should not be used as food. They were the true
Expendables – the flower of their type.
They left their mothers for self-immolation,
The penalty the same for being on
Or off the target – for the first to join
Their own combustion to that of the ships,
And for the second, just to go the way
Their victims went – a drunken headlong spiral,
Shunted from an exhausted radius
Down fifteen thousand feet or more of sea,
Engines, propellers, gyros, rudders, dead.

The S.C. 42 was being groomed
To match a new suspected strategy.
The sleuths till now had surfaced, stabbed and dived
In lone attack. This convoy had to face
The risk of concentrated ambush, meet it
By leaving beaten sea-lanes, east and west,
And in the ambiguity of the wastes
To seek the harsh alliance of the ice
And fog, where Arctic currents were more friendly,
And long nights blanketed the periscopes.

THE CONVOY CONFERENCE

In the Conference room the language dripped with brine.
Veterans, who nearly half a century
Ago had flown their flags on battle cruisers,
Were busy grafting some new sprouts of Gaelic
And Newfie-Irish on an English stump.
They had saluted Fisher as cadets,   2
Heard *Open Fire* under Jellicoe,   3
Outridden typhoons off the Solomons
And at the Falklands cancelled Coronel.   4

154

'Twas time they had a spell of garden peace,
A time to trim their briers and colour Meerschaums.
Those old days were the real days – now, by God
They had to tread the decks of merchantmen,
From flagships to dry cargo-ships and tankers.

THE NAVAL CONTROL SERVICE OFFICER ADDRESSES
THE MASTERS:
"Good morning, gentlemen. It is a pleasure
To see familiar faces here today.
To such of you who have commanded ships
In earlier convoys what I have to say
Will be just dishing up the old instructions.
But since to many it is the first adventure,
I know you'll pardon me if I should cover
With some precision the important points.
Let me begin by saying that your convoy
Has, in its Commodore, one of the most
Renowned men in the Service. It is not
For me to talk at length about his fine
And honourable record. It is known
To all of you. He has of his free choice
Issued from his well-earned retirement
To place at the disposal of the Allies
His knowledge, skill, and practical seamanship.
Here at this table, gentlemen: Rear-Admiral
Sir Francis Horatio Trelawney-Camperdown!

"The Senior Naval Officer will have
Escort and convoy under his command.
An able and distinguished officer,
He is through long and personal experience
Well-versed in enemy tactics, and your safety
Will be the escort's first consideration.

N.C.S.O. THUMBING THE PAGES OF
"GENERAL INSTRUCTIONS"
"Being in all respects ready for sea,
The ships will have steam up and hoist pennants
At daybreak. Note – The Commodore will sound

A prolonged blast. The ships will leave anchorage
In single column and at intervals
Of three minutes, and in the following order,
The Commodore leading . . .
                              You will shorten cables
XX minutes before you heave up. Note —
You will be making seaward on the ebb.
You start two columns after dropping pilots.
Notice in Form A1 all the instructions
Governing matters of sequence, columns and speed.

"May I now draw your most thorough attention
To that important fire page, section B
Of General Instructions (a voice — 'regular page
of bumph');   *that* COMPLETE
BLACKOUT AT NIGHT. Only last week reports
Came in of a ship sunk because she showed
A light, and that despite the most emphatic
Warnings at the conference prior to the sailing.
Remember — have deadlights and scuttles closed,
The blackout curtains checked, no cigarettes
Or pipes lighted on deck and every measure
To conceal the convoy put into effect.

"And likewise of the first significance,
Page 3 at section D concerning 'Smoke'.
Advice is being received of ships making
Black smoke which with good visibility
May be observed for many miles at sea,
And I may add for hours after a convoy
Has passed a given point. I must repeat
This warning — Do not make black smoke in daylight!

"Again. Your route has with the greatest care
Been chosen by the Admiralty experts.
But may I point out that such care and judgment
Could be offset by so simple a matter
As refuse-dumping over rails. Do not —
(Voices — 'Wrap it around the bully beef.'
'No, put it in the soup to give it body.'
'God, that tomato soup needs body and flavour.'

156

'I'd put it in the kye to take the stink out.')
Do NOT throw garbage in the sea in day time.
That's a dead give-away. A crate or carton
Floating astern a convoy might betray
The existence and position of the ships.
That practice must at all cost be avoided.
And most important for internal safety
Of convoy lines is that of station-keeping.
A ship that's not in station is out of control;
The turns in moments of emergency
Cannot successfully be executed,
Unless this measure strictly is observed.
I do not need to emphasize this maxim.

"These measures are of front-line urgency.
W/T silence must always be maintained
Along the route. Occasionally it's broken,
Not wilfully indeed but carelessly,
By operators fresh from the radio school,
Whose fingers have not lost the itch to tap
The keys to break the tedium by listening
To crackle on 500 kilocycles.
A random da da dit dit dit might be
An invitation to the U-boats ready
To accept it. They are ever listening
In on our frequencies and you know well
The manner the Direction Finder Loop
On a surfaced U-boat will follow a signal.
It's like a human ear alerted, which
Will turn to the source of a sound to get a bearing.
You must remember that the enemy
Will not relax his efforts to pick up
Those waves, that German D/F stations even
As far away as Occupied Europe
Are taking bearings, plotting out our ships.

"Now, gentlemen: here is the Commodore."

SIR FRANCIS HORATIO:
"Gentlemen: I shall be very brief and I hope
To be as brief after we get to sea.

I shall keep my signals to a minimum,
But when a hoist DOES go up I shall
Expect immediate acknowledgment.
Many of us have sailed together already,
And gone through several trying situations.
But our success, such as it is, has sprung
From absolute obedience to instructions
And from endurance which must be assumed.
While it is true that for the navigation
Of his own ship each master must be held
Responsible, there is but little room
For rugged individualists. Elsewhere
Perhaps the Nelson touch may be applied,
And a captain's intuitions exercised,
But not within the stations of a convoy.
(Chuckles amongst the older masters.)

"The N.C.S.O. has referred to the matter
Of showing lights. A match, lit on deck, has
Been spotted by an escort at two miles,
And last crossing, a thoughtless biped left
A port open and failed to notice the signal
From a destroyer. It required a burst
From a machine-gun to close it. I am sure
We shall require no such emphasis
In this convoy but I should urge each master
To make the business of lights a top concern,
Particularly at the change of Watch.
Men dropping in to a stuffy galley to make
A mug of tea before going below
Are the principal offenders.
                              Do not wait
Till you are deep in fog before you stream
Your fog-buoys. That is generally too late.
Your next astern by that time has lost touch.
Good seamanship and team-play should prevent
Avoidable collisions in thick fog.

"If you are new to convoy you may be
Tempted to flash on at full brilliancy

Your navigation lights when another ship
Closes you. DON'T. *You are as visible*
To him as he to you. Keep closed up. Keep
Lights dimmed except in an emergency.

"I shall say little here about the stragglers.
The record of the losses says it much
More clearly, and the escort cannot help
You if you leave the family. They are good;
They can work wonders but not miracles.

"And now if you're uncertain of anything —
Emergency turns, for instance — come and have
A chin with me at the close of the conference.
And to repeat, we're in this business all
Together, and in it up to the neck:
For my part, I am bloody proud of it.
Good morning, gentlemen, and a good voyage."

N.C.S.O.:
"Questions?"

CHORUS: *"Plenty."*

HARVEY BUTT: *"I'm in the wrong position.*
Too far astern. I have a 12-knot ship.
I want a place in first or second line
To save me bumpin' into 6-knot tramps."

JIM BURDOCK:
"This convoy got no tramps."

BUTT: *"Well, all I know*
The last one had 'em, and I knocked the sterns
Off three of them, and I was always goin'
Full speed astern to save my goddam neck."

"JOHN KNOX" O'FLAHERTY:
"I could make 8 knots if I didn't have
Such lousy coal. The bloody stuff won't steam.
A half of it is gravel — wouldn't boil
A kettle: looks like salvage from a wreck
Picked up from sweepings left on Sable Island."

159

CHARLIE SHIPSIDE:
"And I don't like my place – gummed up between
A couple of tankers. God, if I'm not fished
I'll be run down."

JACK DOUCETTE: *"Why should I be back there?*
Never did like the stern of columns. Suppose
I'm in there just for picking up survivors.
What do you take me for – an ambulance?"

JERRY PAYNE:
"8 knots would tear the guts out of my tub.
I haven't had a refit for three years.
Can't execute a turn of forty-five degrees.
We'll be colliding every fifteen seconds."

ROBERT FITZSIMMONS:
"My pumps were out of gear when she was built;
Still out of gear; complained a hundred times,
But can't get any action."

MICHAEL SALTAWAY: *"I have this*
To say. I only got one boiler workin';
And that one's on half-time – the other half
Is restin' – and I've only half a crew."

NORWEGIAN CAPTAIN, LEANING HEAVILY ON NATIVE
SPEECH:
"I kan ikke forstaa fordommt ord.
How in helvete tink dey dat I kan
Faa 8 knots ut of my old vaskelbalja.
Har ikke hatt fullt mannskap for two year.
I lar mig fan ikke fortelle what I
Skal do. You go helvete alle mann."

N.C.S.O.:
"What did he say?"

'ARRY STUBBINS: *" 'E says the bleedin' hinstructions*
Are fine and quite clear to 'is hunderstandin'."

ROBIN MACALLISTER:
"Nae, nae, he canna' thole thae English turrms.

160

He'd ken a' richt, gin you gae him the Gaelic.
I wad respeckfully suggest the wurrds
O' the Genneral Instructions be convairted
Into a ceevilized tongue so that a chiel
Micht hae nae doots. Noo, let me spik mi thochts."

(Voices: "Now, what did HE say?" "Noo's the day
and noo's the hour." "Is this St. Andrew's Night?"
"Pipe in the haggis.")

A DANISH CAPTAIN:
"No, no. He sess he do not IKKE know
One word. His vaskelbalja — tub-tub, washtub,
Das iss he mean his ship, can't make 8 knots.
No crew MANNSKAP full up for long long time.
Ship had no refit since she left Bergen
In 1894. He tol' me dat
Himself. He not quite clear. He sess ve can
All go to hella. Don't care damn.
                                        I got
Complaints ALSO. Want get dem off my chest.
Goddam nuisance, I seh, dose para-a-vanes.
Muss up de vurks. Crew don't like dem damn bit.
Dey seh put hex on ship — a buncha Jonahs.
And more ALSO I seh. No compass checks.
Dose D/G coils play hell wid compasses.
De gear get loose on deck. Dey come adrift."

CYRUS BUMSTEAD:
"I don't want anyone to tell me how
To run my ship — been in the Services,
Merchant and Navy, nigh come forty years.
I was a Master when the most of them
Were spottin' patterns on their diapers."

MARK KNEE TO CYRUS:
"I squeezed the Atlantic from my mitts before
Those Juniors had their birthday buttons on."

CAPTAIN, THE HONOURABLE GUY BRIMBLECOMBE:
"Well, sir, you needn't worry about MY ship.
She went through this before: she'll go again.

161

She's in good trim. I have a splendid crew.
Signals will be acknowledged to the letter,
And in the sea tradition, I assure you."

N.C.S.O.:
"Now, gentlemen, since it is quite apparent
That we are all in utmost harmony
On the main grounds, it is just left for me
To wish 'good-luck'. Never have I attended
A Conference where there was such fine feeling
Combined with insight and rare technical grasp
Of the problems of a convoy operation.
Let me congratulate you. May I now
Invite you, on behalf of a great friend
Of the R.C.N., to the Periwinkle Club
At Lobster Point where you may hoist a couple
To take the chill from the September fog."

*   *   *   *   *

In a few hours from the time the blinds
Were drawn upon the jags and the last lisp   8
Against the universe and things marine
Was but a reminiscence lapsed in rum,
Those men were on the Bridge peering through fog
And moving towards their ordered rendezvous.

*   *   *   *   *

One half a million tons were in the holds,
Cramming to the last precious cubic inch
The slow-keeled merchantmen – the sixty-six.
No longer were those ships an industry
Run for peacetime returns upon investment.
They took their line positions for defence.
Against them mainly was the warfare waged –
Bulk cargo carriers with box-like sections,
Ship side to ship side and the main deck to keel,
Carrying their gross of ore and coal and grain;
The ships with 'tween decks running the full length;
Tankers equipped with special pumps for oil;

Refrigeration ships, holds insulated
For storage of the perishable goods;
And hybrid types that had their bellies full
Of oranges, aluminum and lint.

How desperate the strait which would commit
A treasure of this price to such a journey!
Where find a steward who would risk his name
To close the page of such accountancy
When every mile along the ocean highway
Was calling for protection, and in calling
Demanded life and life's expenditure?
And here the call was answered with a guard
Whose substitute for numbers was its courage —
Four terriers slipped from the Canadian kennel:
But one destroyer, *Skeena*; three corvettes,
Kenogami, Orillia and *Alberni.*
Upon their vigil hung the life of all,
Of ships and men. Of sleeker, faster breed,
The *Skeena* ranged a far periphery
At thirty knots, now out of sight and now
Closing the convoy as her nose tried out
The dubious scents in narrowing ellipses.
The slower guards kept closer to their broods,
Pushing their way within the column lanes,
Emerged to pace the port and starboard flanks
Or nuzzled with a deep strategic caution
The hulls of those whose tardy engine beats
Brought down the knots of faster ships and made
The gravest risk and worry for the fleet.
They kept a special watch upon the tankers.
No ships, no aeroplanes, no jeeps could stir
Without this source of power and lubrication.
Even the merchantmen must flank these ships,
Herded like buffalo young inside the ring.

*   *   *   *   *

COMMODORE TO SIGNALMAN:
"Signal to pennants 73, relay   9
To pennants 103, Stop Pouring Smoke!"

163

INTERNAL MURMURINGS:
"Look at it tossin' like a Texas twister.
That smoke is blacker than an Afghan's whiskers.
I'd like to tell that Captain of the Heads
He should have stayed at home with the kind of job
That suited him — housebreakin' his Angoras."

OFFICIAL:
"And pennants 114 is out of station."

UNOFFICIAL:
"That flappin' penguin from the Auckland Islands
Has been a week on route, yet needs more time
To get rid of that Newfie-Crowsnest screech.
He'll lose it when he's doused. Get back in station,
For if you don't, the canaries will stop singin'."

THE MASTER'S THOUGHTS:
"I told those sculpins at the conference
I couldn't make that eight — a half a knot
Above a six would blow my stinkin' boilers.
I haven't had a cleanin' for a year,
And there's a beach of sand inside the gears,
And yet that bargee yells — GET BACK IN STATION!"

COMMODORE:
"And pennants 74 by the Diet of Worms!
He's waddlin' like an old barnyard merganser.
Another hour by the way he's goin'
He'll be out on the flanks duckin' his feathers,
Or lost in fog and stragglin' back to Sydney.
Keep pumpin' Morse into his ruddy blinkers."

THE MASTER IN QUESTION:
"I've got a twisted rudder — like a corkscrew,
And if that poopin' punk there on that flagship
Imagines he's Paul Bunyan or the devil,
Tell him put on his shorts and straighten it."

10

P.O. TO GALLEY-BOY:
"Gallagher, did your mother tell you nothin'
On the way home? Stop pitchin' gash in daytime.

Handin' the convoy on a platter to the subs.
As bad as smoke to give the trail away.
Just one more bad tomato over there,
And all the ships will quit this lovely Service,
And you'll go with the galley, do you hear?"

GALLAGHER:
"Why won't that windpipe slitter tell me what
I got to do with all that mouldy gash?
'Twas gash when it was brought aboard, 'twas gash
When it was crated; now it's maggoty.
Can't eat it and can't burn it and can't dump it.
I'd like to foul his beak in those tomatoes."

North of the sixtieth, they had, it seemed,
Found refuge in a sea-berth where the foe,
Finding the chill enter his crop, might seek
More southern fodder. Least of all the hazards
Were winds and waves: for these the ships were built.
Their bows could bull the heavier seas head-on.
Their hulls could stand the shock beam-to. The keels
Had learned the way to bite into the troughs:
Such was their native element. The acts
Of God were taken as their daily fare
Received alike with prayers or curses. These
Were as the dice fell – whether luck of devil
Or luck of God spilled on a shifting floor
Close to the steady fringe of the Arctic Circle.

For seven days and nights without attack!
The asdic operator in his hut
Had sent his ultra-sounds out and reported
Echoes, but only such as might return
As the dull, soft reverberation notes
From seaweed or low forms of ocean life
Or from a school of porpoises or whales.
His hearing was as vital to the ship
As was the roving sight in a crowsnest.

His ear was as the prism is to light,
Unravelling meanings from a skein of tone.

Each sound might hold a threat, a Bremen slur,
An overture to a dementia
Of guns and rockets and torpedo hits
Competing with the orders from the Bridge.
He had to know that threat and not mistake it.
For that his body was a sounding-board.
Even his knees must feel it and his face
Become a score for undetermined notes,
As if a baton in his cortex played
Wry movements on his neurones fiddle-taut,
Twitched his reflexes into spasms, narrowed
His pupils, kicked his heart into his throat.

He had an instrument in his control
Attested by the highest signatures of science.
The echoes had traversed wide spans of time: —
Helmholtz and Doppler tapping to each other   12
Through laboratory walls, and there was Rayleigh
Calling to Langevin, he to Fresnel,
The three hymning Pindarics to Laplace,
And all vibrating from their resonators
Salutes to Robert Boyle, halloos to Newton.
And here, his head-phones on, this operator,
Sleeve-rolled mechanic to the theorists,
Was holding in his personal trust, come life,
Come death, their cumulative handiwork.
Occasionally a higher note might hit
The ear-drum like a drill, bristle the chin,
Involving everything from brain to kidneys,
Only to be dismissed as issuing
From the submerged foundations of an iceberg,
Or classified as "mutual interference".

The hopes were running higher the farther north
The convoy steamed. Would this one get its break?
The Arctic pressed into the human service,
The Circle which had caught the navigators —
The hardiest in the annals of The Search,
Willoughby, Chancelor, Hudson, Bering, Franklin —   13
Impounded them, twisted and broken them,

166

Their ships and crews upon its icy spokes:
This time through the ironic quirk of War
Changed to an allied *cordon sanitaire*.

The evening of the eighth day and a moon,
High-sailing and impersonal, picked out
The seventy ships, deriding the constrained
Hush of the blackout. Was the latitude
Itself not adequate watch? The sea was calm,
Although with a beam swell the wallowing rate
Was but five knots. The moon illuminated
The *Empire Hudson*, leader of port wing,
Loaded with grain, the *Gypsum Queen* with sulphur,
The *Winterswyck*, the *Garm*, the *Scania*,
Muneric (iron ore – sink like a rock
She would if hit), *Bretwalda*, *Baron Ramsay*,
Gullpool, the *Empire Panther* and *Macgregor*,
The *Lorient*, *Arosa*, *Hampton Lodge*,
And others with the same high names and pennants,
Carrying at the load-water line their freight –
Twelve columns of them in their blueprint stations.
A half an hour to dusk the bo'sun's mate
Had piped his strictest order – *Darken Ship*.

Thousands of sailors under decks were sealed
As in vast envelopes. They ate and worked
And slept within a world self-quarantined
Against the pestilence of light by bolts,
Bulkheads and battened portholes, for each cell
Was like a tumoured brain, danger within,
Danger without, divided from the world
By an integument of iron bone.
What chance for life the moment when a shell
Trepanned the skull? What would release the pressure
Of that stampede to reach the for'ard hatch –
That burial hole in the deckhead – and come up
When the plates buckled in the lower mess?
Danger within? Could not the magazines
By a raffle flirt of fate be made to turn
Against the convoy, striking through the escort,

167

With final undeliberated measure,
When the oil tanks would join the magazines
To the last ton, to the last gram of blunder?
The fires that warmed the galleys could cremate:
For oil and fulminate of mercury,
Nitrated cellulose and T.N.T.
And the constituents of our daily bread,
Fresh water and fresh air, could by a shift,
Sudden and freakish in the molecules,
Be transubstantiated into death.

Added to this might come the blows where friend
Struck friend with utmost shoulder energy –
Blows just as murderous as torpedo hits
Where in the darkness, executing turns,
Or in the fog, the convoy ships would find
Their plates as vulnerable as cellophane:
Or from excess of their protective zeal
The fighting units with their double rate
Of convoy speed might plough their sinuous way
Up through the narrow lanes and turn too sharp,
Presenting their full beams across the bows
Of leading merchantmen. Lucky they were
If they escaped with nothing but a blast
Of roaring basso from the Commodore's lungs –
"Those lousy, noisy, nattering sons o' badgers,
Where do they think they're going – to Miami,
Harpooning porpoises or flying fish?"

The Silent Service never won its name
With fairer title than it did this night.
Evening at half-past nine and a fresh sound,
An instant octave lift to treble pitch
From the dull datum of "reverbs" startled
The ear. *"An echo bearing* GREEN FOUR-O,
Range 1500."
        "Hold and classify."
The *ping-g-g* with its death's head identity!

C.O. TO OFFICER-OF-WATCH:
"Increase speed 250 revolutions."

14

(Officer-of-the-Watch repeats, calls down voice-pipe to coxswain who sets engine-room telegraph to speed. The Engineer Officer-of-Watch acknowledges. His chief E.R.A.[15] swings wheel-throttle-valve open to make required revolutions. Engine-room telegraph confirms to wheelhouse and coxswain calls up voice-pipe – *"Wheelhouse-Bridge: 250 revolutions on, sir."* Bridge Officer-of-Watch repeats to captain.)

The *Skeena* heeled to port on *"starboard ten"*
To keep the target on the bow. *"Steady
On* TWO-FOUR-SEVEN.*"* (Harry one at the dip.)
"Left cut on TWO-FOUR-SIX. . . . *Right cut
On* TWO-FIVE-THREE.*"* (Reporting Doppler)
"Echo high and inclination closing."
The range 1200. *"Target moving right:
Centre bearing,* TWO-FIVE-FIVE.*"*
One thousand yards: *"extent of target – ten."*

Not ice this time but moving steel submerged –
Two hundred feet of longitudinal plate,
Forged at the Krupp's and tested in the Baltic,
Were answering the taps.
                    "Stand by depth-charges."

CAPTAIN TO CHIEF YEOMAN:
*"Take an emergency report to shore:
'In contact with classified submarine'."*
(Chief Yeoman repeats to W.T. office.)
A crackle of Morse, and in bare space of seconds
The warning goes to Admiralty, from there
To allied ships in threatened area,
And on the walls in *Operations,* where
The swastikas and shadows of the U-boats
Follow in replica the Atlantic movements,
A red peg moves along the chart to plot
The first of the disease spots that would pock
The body of the S.C. 42.

Whatever doubt the eye might have imposed
Upon the ear soon vanished with the signals.

Jedmore reported two torpedoes passed
Ahead. *Muneric*, fourth ship in port column,
Attacked, dragged instantly, sank with her iron.
The Commodore – *"Saw U-boat on port bow."*
Kenogami in contact with another,
A third, a fourth. Suspicions which had wormed
Their way along the vine were proved. The first
Wolf-pack engagement of the Atlantic War
Was on! A fifth . . . a seventh! They had trailed
The ships to Greenland waters. Moonlight full,
Without the mercy of clouds, had turned
A traitor to the convoy, cancelling
The northern length of nights. Like teal not yet
Surprised to wing, the silhouetted ships
Awaited leisured barrels from the hunters,
And the warheads drilled them as from open sights.

Orillia, detailed to sweep astern,
Picked up the few survivors, took in tow
The S.S. *Tachee*, badly hit but still
Afloat: rockets were seen in midst of convoy:
A signal from the flagship – " *'Empire Hudson'*
Torpedoed on port side." The triple task –
To screen the convoy, counter-attack, and then,
The humane third of rescuing the sailors,
Seemed far beyond the escort's hope or effort.
To save to kill, to kill to save, were means
And ends closely and bloodily allied.
Hundreds of sailors un-lifejacketed
Clawed at the jetsam in the oil and water.
Captains and Commodore were well aware
Of how a lame one in a chase could spatter
With blood the entire herd. High strategy
Demanded of the brain an execution
Protested by the tactics of the heart.
And there was only half an inch or less
Of a steel skin upon the escort's hulls –
Not for self-safety were those ships designed.
Just here the log with its raw elements

Enshrined a saga in a phrase of action.
"The 'Empire Hudson' listing badly, crew
And officers were disembarked. Someone
Reported – 'Secret papers have not been
Destroyed, mersigs, swept-channels, convoy route,
And codes, the CODES!' And as there was a chance
The steamer might not sink, 'Kenogami'
Was ordered to embark an officer,
Return him to the listed deck to find
And sink the weighted papers – which was done."
This stark undecorated phrase was just
An interlinear item in the drama,
Three words spelling a deed unadvertised,
When ships announced their wounds by rockets, wrote
Their own obituaries in flame that soared
Two hundred feet and stabbed the Arctic night
Like some neurotic and untimely sunrise.
Exploding tankers turned the sky to canvas,
Soaked it in orange fire, kindled the sea,
Then carpeted their graves with wreaths of soot.
The sea would tidy up its floor in time,
But not just now, – gaskegs and rafts and mops,
Oilskins, sou'westers, sea-boots, duffel coats
Drifted above the night's burnt offerings.
Only the names remained uncharred – *Muneric,*
Ulysses, Baron Pentland, Sally Maersk,
The *Empire Crossbill, Empire Hudson, Stargard –*
Merely heroic memories by morning.

The early hours of daylight drove the subs
To cover though the escort knew that eyes,
As sleepless as their own but unobserved
Behind the grey-green mesh of swell and lop,
Were following the convoy's desperate plunge.
All knew that no restrictive rules would hedge
This fight: to the last ship, to the last shot,
To the last man, for fair was foul and foul
Was fair in that *mêlée* of strength and cunning.
Tirpitz and Fisher thirty years before

Had scanned the riddles in each other's eyes.
What was the argument about the belt
That drained the sophistry of principles
Inside a ring? *"Hit first, hit hard, hit fast!"*
Tirpitz had trumped him with — *"Hit anywhere."*   17
And here today only one point was certain —
Sailors above the sea, sailors below,
Drew equally upon a fund of courage.
No one might gamble on the other's fear
Or waning will, Commander Schmidt might flood
His tanks and dive when something on his mirror
Called for discretion, but in his own shrewd time
He could be reckoned on to blow the ballast
And frame that picture on the glass again.
He would come up with Botterschult and Rickert,
Von Braundorff, Niebergall, Schippmann and Fritzsche.
They knew their crews would never fail the switches
Or rush the conning towers before the orders,
Though the depth-charges pounded the blood vessels,
Though combing rams just missed them overhead.
In what proportions did the elements
Combine to move those individual pawns
Of power in their massed flesh-and-nerve formation
Across a board? Grit human; bruinine;
Habits that would not heckle a command,
Obedience that sealed the breach of fear,
A frenzy that would spurn the slopes of Reason
Under a rhetoric of Will which placed
Before the *herrenvolk* historic choices —
To scramble up a cliff and vandalize
The sunlight or else perish on the ledges.

These were the enemies the convoy fronted:
Metal to metal, though in this arena
The odds lay heavily with the pursuers,
Even by day — for what were periscopes
At distance of three thousand yards, that reared
Their tiny heads curved like swamp moccasins?
What was their smothered wake compared with that

172

Propeller wash, that height and drift of smoke,
Those lines of funnels with their sixty hulls?
And so it was a safe bet on the sub
When at high noon one left her nest and sped
Her charge right at the S.S. *Thistleglen*,
Dead at the waterline and full amidships.
It took three minutes for the merchantman
To dock her pigiron on the ocean floor.

"There, there he is!"

               Seven cables from the spot
Where suction swirled above the foundering,
The periscope light-grey – one minute only!
The *Skeena* carried out a pounce attack
Of ten depth-charges fired with shallow settings.
The asdic trailed the sub proceeding north
At three-knot speed. *Kenogami* confirmed
Echoes. Depth-charges with deep settings dropped,
The echoes ceased, and a great patch of oil
Surfaced, and a huge bubble like a blister
Broke, close to the position of explosions.
"This time for keeps we pinged his bloody hide, sir:
We've sent him down to join the 'Thistleglen'."

With this by day, what could another night
Not call forth from the cupboard? Afternoon
Wore on till dusk with that dramatic lull
Which acted like narcotics on the heart,
Yet put high-tension circuits in the brain.

"The 'Sally Maersk' went down with bread enough
To feed an army for a month."

                   "But what
A job the corvettes did in rescuing
Them all – the fifty-four under that fire."
"Most of the 'Baron Pentland' too."

                       "Her back
Was broken though her lumber kept her floating."

Could the same chance be taken the next night?
An hour after nightfall and the convoy

Had pierced the sixty-second parallel.
Twelve shortened columns tightened up their gaps,
All ships under instructions – (You will not – repetition –
Not break W.T. silence without deep suspicion of
U-boat presence.)   Owing to moon
Rear ships of the port column were instructed
To drop smoke floats should enemy appear
On the port side. Each minute passed, each mile
Northward were credit items on a ledger.
And now quickening the heart, two friendly shadows,
Corvettes, steamed into shape – *Moose Jaw, Chambly* –
Two added to the four. But still the hope
Was on evasion – on the North – to kick
Them with their wounded heels and merge the spoors
Within the Greenland-Iceland ocean tundras.
And so the last night's vigil was repeated,
Although more ominous the silences:
More broken, too, the sleep as the ears buzzed
Still with the dental burr of the point-fives,   18
And the yellow cordite from the four-point-sevens   19
Kept up its smart under exhausted eyelids.
The average rate was lowered by three knots.
The *Tachee* was in tow of the *Orillia*,
Fumbling her rudder. From the *Chambly*'s deck,
Two miles away, the ships seemed fated targets.
Silent and slow and dark as, clothed with crape,
They journeyed on like mourners, having left
The Saxon burial of their sister ships,
And bearing on themselves the same contagion.
The air was breathing out its prophecy.
So was the water. There was mockery
Within the sea's caress – the way a wave
Would clamber up the bow of the *Moose Jaw*, scout
Around the shadows of the foc's'le,
Tattoo the face of the Bridge and lazily
Slither along the deck and then hiss through
The hawse-pipes as the corvette dipped her nose
To the slow anaesthetic of the swell.
Mockery it was on face and lips and fingers,

For, after her reconnaissance, the sea,
As urging death with a forensic fury,
Would shed her velvet syllables, return
With loaded fists to thunder at the gun-shields,
Trying to crack defence before the battle
Was joined between the "patterns" and the "tubes".   20

Eleven-thirty, and the navigator,
His coat and boots on in his bunk, completes
A nightmare with a steady mumbling curse.
He thought the order was *Abandon Ship* –
It was an O.D. calling Middle Watch.
He wakes, turns over, and again turns over,
Yawns, stretches and turns out, proceeds to Bridge,
Peers through the blackout curtains, and in dim
Blue battle-light he squints and notes night orders,
The toughest order of the toughest Watch
(Maintain tail sweep from two to four thousand yards).

He focuses binoculars to range
The horizon arcs. *"A lot of whales about
Tonight."* The echoes picked them up. Four hours!
He has to fight that Middle Watch fatigue,
And as the minutes crawl he sucks life-savers,
Or cracks one on his teeth for company.
A line of spray leaps up above the dodger
And like rawhide cuts him across the face.
Then, too, that phosphorescence on the sea
Is easily mistaken in its darts,
Flashes and curves for what the lookout fears.
Two hours are gone: another two to go.
(That wrist-watch ticks off hours instead of seconds.)
His eyelids blink to ease the strain that falls
Like mist upon a telescopic lens.
A starboard lookout yell jerks back his senses –
"Torpedo bearing green-four-O." Lookout
Recoils from an expected blow that does
Not strike. *"Damn porpoises: they always home
In on the bow."*
(*The navigating officer wipes the sweat from his forehead*

with his sleeve, tells the sub-lieutenant to take over for a
few minutes as he wants to go to Heads. Then he calls to
a stand-by.)
                    "Say, Spinney, what about
A mug of kye?"
                    "Yes, Sir."
                              Spinney had not
Yet found his legs. Less than six months before
He had been learning Latin and the class-
Room smell had not been kippered from his system.
To him the ocean was a place of travel,
A blue-green oriental boulevard
Round unknown continents – up to this year;
And even to last night the illusion stayed,
When for his benefit the Borealis
Staged a rehearsal of the Merry Dancers
Before the blood-red footlights till it paled
The myth upon a tracery of starshell.
He now goes to the galley, fills a jug
With kye, picks up a half a dozen mugs,
Stumbles, skates, splashes half of it on deck.
Some drops of rain and sea-foam tincture it.
Along the way a leading-hand of the Watch
And a rheumatic coder cadge a drink,
And by the time that Spinney finds his balance
On the bridge only a soapy seawash greets
The navigator's throat. *"What in the name*
Of all buck goats is this? Where did you get
This swill?" (He hands it to the sub to drink.)
                              "Go back and fill her up again,
And keep her clean."
                              Spinney steps down from bridge,
Staggers, makes for the ladder, cracks the jug
Against the signal-box before he slides,
Reaches the galley and returns, tries hard
To wean his legs from the quadrangle walk,
Does a Blue Danube on the deck, and then
Revokes his quondam heroes (what a bunch
Of fools those ancients were to travel,

176

Aeneas was the biggest ass on earth!)
And flinging out his last accusative
At what is limned on the horizon, he
Remeasures his Virgilian cadences
In terms of stresses gliding queasily
Along the black ramps of the North Atlantic.

At ten to four Lieutenant Snell takes over,
And the two victims of the Watch slope down
With brains of fog and eyes of fractured glass.
Their legs go aft by instinct to their bunks,
Their minds well in advance entering a coma
Beyond gun-cotton shock or Gabriel's horn.

'Twas only in a stupor that O'Leary
Recalled his reprimand. When did it happen?
"Yeoman, you dropped no markers with that pattern.
That's standing orders now — smoke-floats to mark
Areas attacked. Ever heard it? Don't you know
Your drill? You'll be in my report in the morning."
O'Leary gagged upon his chewing quid,
Hiccuped, sending a spurt of nicotine
And hydrochloric acid on the sea.
"He said to me, said he, 'O'Leary, don't
You know your drill?' — Say, how the hell would I know?
Nobody tells me nothing in this Navy."

A bo'sun caught the Peggy with a fag.
"Cripes, do you want to bitch this midnight show?
That lighted butt is visible for miles,
And on the starboard wing, too. Don't you know
The one and only moral law of Moses
Is never light a fag on deck at night?
A law you got to learn while in the Service.
A light can be machine-gunned by the escort.
They'd ping your fag and teeth at the same time."

PEGGY, OUT OF EARSHOT:
"I didn't light it on the deck. I cupped
My hands and took three drags and that was all.
That jockey groomed for donkeys thinks he's got

177

The whole world by the tail in a down pull.
When I get back to Civvy Street, I'll call him."

O'Meara, Steele and Casey had a lot
To say. They'd gab it when the day came round –
The day the *Stargard* reached her port – but somehow
The water and the salt got in their throats
The moment when the *Stargard* took them under.

The dark was sedative and irritant.
How easy was it for an interval
To muffle the senses with a hushed blackout,
And the diminuendo of the run
Could well delude the reason. This was not
The rate that marked the fever of pursuit,
And nothing from the decks was visible
To show the way the trimmest escort unit
Could be in shackles to a lubber keel,
And have to be replaced in precious moments;
Nothing to show how gyros and magnetics
Could be ungeared by submarine explosions.
For this was information undiffused
Among the crew or countered by illusions,
Or by resumption of the normal tasks.
No one from the *Ulysses* lived to cite
The witness of the E.R.A.s and firemen,
Pounding the steel rungs in that inner trap
When the torpedo struck her gas and oil.

The drama of the night before was over.
No headlines would record as news the toil,
As stokers every hour took temperatures
Of bearings, scribbled them on pads, transferred
Them to the logs and then resumed their rounds
To watch for popping valves, to check the flow
By turning wheels when the full head of steam
Was hitting the square inches of the boilers.
There was no spotlight on the items when
A leading seaman of the watch reported
"The temperature of the sea forty degrees,
The lowering falls are clear, boats off the pins,

The watertight compartments are all closed."
No one would mould the linotype for such
A mass that might survive or not survive
Their tedium of watches in the holds –
The men with surnames blotted by their jobs
Into a scrawl of anonymity.
A body blow at the boilers would untype
All differentiations in the blood
Of pumpmen, wipers, messmen, galley boys
Who had become incorporate with the cogs
On ships that carried pulp and scrap to Europe.

Desire invoking for the memory
Amnesia for the nightmare that had passed,
It might have been a run in peaceful times.
The sounds seemed casual enough – lookouts
Reporting to the officers on watch,
Got back the usual laconic answers.
The turbine notes ran up from *C* to *G*
And down according to the scale of speed.
The scraps of speech from duffel-coated forms,
Huddled beneath the after-canopy,
Had by tacit agreement in the eyes
Nothing to do with present urgencies.
A rating "in the rattle" salved his mind
By giving his opinion of a buffer,
Casting suspicion on the buffer's birth
And pedigree. His *b*'s and *g*'s and *s*'s,
Delivered through his teeth in confidence
To the high winds and seas from A-gun deck,
Had all the symptoms of a normal trip.
Only the action-station gongs could jar
That gentle wishful thinking – and they did.

Horse-power to the limit on the engines,
Levied for scout assault and close defence,
Was routed quickly to defence, for short
Beyond believing was the interval
Between the echoes and torpedo hits,
Between them and the spotted periscopes.

21

179

The Commodore reported, " '*Gypsum Queen*'
Torpedoed and sunk." *Alberni* gets an echo,
Five hundred yards, *Kenogami* confirming.
Chambly and *Moose Jaw* get a definite kill
With prisoners, and then a "probable".
The peril of the night before was doubled.
This time the subs had dived within the convoy,
"*Attacking from within the lines*" – the fear
Above all fears, for, out to sea, the lairs
Might be discerned and the protective screens
Be interposed between them and the convoy.
But now the hazards of the fight were weighted
In favour of the foe. Seven or eight
Out of the estimated twelve were there
Inside or hanging on to flank or rear.
Even blindly they could not miss – on port
And starboard bow, amidships, on the quarter.

Upon the *Skeena*'s Bridge the judgment fought
With chaos. Blindness, deafness visited
The brain. Through a wild paradox of sight
And sound, the asdic echoes would not fall
Within their ribbon-tidy categories.
They bounded in confusion from the hulls
Of tankers and corvettes: the ash-can sounds
Were like those of explosions from torpedoes.
Wake-echoes and reverbs, and *quenching* caused
By pitch and roll of a heavy following sea,
Had blended with the sharper pings from steel
To give the effect of a babel and a brawl.

But blindness was the worst. To find the foe
By starshell served indeed to spot the target,
But carved in white the escort's silhouette.
The need called for the risk. A megaphone
Informed the *Skeena* that a sub was seen
Between the columns seven and eight, its course
Marked by a steady hail of tracer bullets.
The *Skeena* tried to ram; the sub escaped
To an adjacent lane and turned right angles

180

In opposite direction to destroyer.
The shelter of the dark was now a threat
Holding collision as the convoy ships
Made their sharp turn of forty-five degrees.
Her fighting and her navigating lights
Were switched on to identify the *Skeena*,
Scratching the paint upon the merchant hulls,
As orders pelted down the voice-pipe, helm
And engines answering – *"Full speed ahead ...*
Starboard twenty ... Stop both ... Half-ahead port ...
Half-astern starboard ... Stop starboard ...
Half-ahead starboard ... Full ahead both ..."

This was infighting at its grisly worst.
The issue grew more leaden as the night
Advanced, and what relief could daylight offer
Against the weary arithmetic count?
The *Winterswyck* blown up, sunk with her phosphate;
Stonepool torpedoed on both sides, gone down
With general cargo and a fleet of trucks.
And matching the confusion on the decks
Was the confusion in the ether, ships
Torpedoed, burning, sinking, hammering out
Their cryptocodes. What listeners could sort them,
Solve those recurring decimals of dots
And those long dashes when the operators
Screwed down the keys – their last official acts –
To give the drowning wails of instruments?
What rescuers could hurry to position?
Only the fighting ships – and they were fighting.

"Which one was that?"
                        "A tanker bad enough,
But not as bad as that; a flame that would
Frizzle a glacier."
                        "Aviation gas?"

"It could create that light but not that roar,
'Twould cause stokehold concussion miles away,
And wake up Julianehaab."   22
                        " 'Twas ammunition."

The *Garm* and *Scania* with their lumber lost!
Rockets observed from *Randa* and *Benury* –
The signals ceased – both missing in the morning!

The fourteen sunk and others just afloat,
The remnant staggered on still north-by-east.

*   *   *   *   *

Last night, the second night, and must there come
A third? The ratio of loss had climbed
Beyond all normal fears. The logs themselves
Might not be legible on that third morning.
So far the tale was grim enough – but six
Saved of the *Jedmore*'s crew; eight from the *Stonepool*;
Less than half from the *Garm*; six from the *Stargard*;
Two from the *Winterswyck*; and a great blank –
The fate of crew unknown – was logged for *Scania,*
The *Empire Springbuck, Crossbill, Thistleglen,*
Muneric and *Ulysses*. The third night
To come! Those hammerheads were off there still,
Hiding, biding. How many? How those freighters
Foundered! How fast? Minutes or seconds?

"Did

You see the way the 'Crossbill' took her dive?
Her cargo steel, she went down like a gannet."

"The 'Muneric' beat her to it. A life-belt
Would have no chances in that suction-hole,
Say nothing of a man. I saw her blades
Rise, edge themselves against the 'Alberni' gunfire."

Why should those phobias of speed, colour
And shape belonging to the night alone
Return to plague the mind in open daylight?
Would those fires start again? A chemistry
That would incinerate its own retort
Raged round the *Stonepool* when she sank. Water
And fire, water and oil, blood, fire and salt
Had agonized their journey through nerve-endings

182

To char themselves upon a graphite-grey
Precipitate. Survivors from the *Stargard*,
Who would for life carry their facial grafts,
Told of the scramble from the boiler rooms,
Up canted ladders and the reeling catwalks,
Only to find their exit was the sea,
And there to find their only exit from
Its cauldron surface was its drowning depth.
Where find the straws to grasp at in this sea?
Where was the cause which once had made a man
Disclaim the sting of death? What ecstasy
Could neutralize this salt and quench this heat
Or open up in victory this grave?
But oil and blood were prices paid for blood
And oil. However variable the time,
The commerce ever was in barter. Oil
Propelled the ships. It blew them up. The men
Died oil-anointed as it choked the *"Christ!"*
That stuttered on their lips before the sea
Paraded them as crisps upon her salver.
This was the payment for the oil designed
To sleek the gears and punch the pistons in
And over Alamein and Normandy.
And blood mixed with the sea-foam was the cost
Of plasma safely carried in the holds
Across an ocean to a continent,
There to unblanch the faces on the fields,
There to revein the vines for fresher fruits
In a new harvest on a hoped tomorrow;
And over all, the purchase of the blood
Was that an old dishonoured postulate,
Scrubbed of its rust, might shine again – *Granted*
That what the mind may think, the tongue may utter.

*   *   *   *   *

Three morning hours were gone and no attack.
Were the U-boats destroyed or shaken off
Or still awaiting night? What mattered it?
What mattered the rotation of the earth?

The clock had struck in seasons those two nights,
And Time was but a fiddler off his key,
Treading the youth through middle age towards death.

From the lookout a signal – *Smoke ahead!*
Was it a surface raider? This would mean
Extinction, still another word for sleep.
The smoke took shape – five funnels pouring it.
Binoculars from the crowsnests and bridges
Of all the ships, escort and convoy, swept
The horizon: dots turned into lines, the lines
To hulls and decks and guns and turrets – five
British destroyers making thirty knots.
This was the restoration for the hearts
Of fifty ships – the maimed, the blind, the whole.
Around them raced the fighters, plotting out
Suspicious zones whenever asdic sweeps
Reported doubtful contacts, searching far
Afield, then closing to resume position
On screen. And so the S.C. 42,
With mutilated but with fashioned columns,
Covered the lap across the Denmark Strait
With that same chivalry of knots which meant
Rescue for hundreds in the Greenland battle.
For with the battered *Tachee* still in tow
Of the *Orillia*, they reached the two
Most northern outposts of the Old World havens,
Rock-armoured Hvalfjord and Reykjavik,
Then took their southern stretch until the convoy
Sighted Inishtrahull and there dispersed.
And the fighting ships, miraculously unscathed,
Proceeded to Moville, to Lishahally,
Thence up the winding Foyle to seek their berths
Around the crowded docks of Londonderry.

Towards the Last Spike

It was the same world then as now – the same,
Except for little differences of speed
And power, and means to treat myopia
To show an axe-blade infinitely sharp
Splitting things infinitely small, or else
Provide the telescopic sight to roam
Through curved dominions never found in fables.
The same, but for new particles of speech –
Those algebraic substitutes for nouns
That sky cartographers would hang like signboards
Along the trespass of our thoughts to stop
The stutters of our tongues with their equations.

As now, so then, blood kept its ancient colour,
And smoothly, roughly, paced its banks; in calm
Preserving them, in riot rupturing them.
Wounds needed bandages and stomachs food:
The hands outstretched had joined the lips in prayer –
"Give us our daily bread, give us our pay."
The past flushed in the present and tomorrow
Would dawn upon today: only the rate
To sensitize or numb a nerve would change;
Only the quickening of a measuring skill
To gauge the onset of a birth or death
With the precision of micrometers.
Men spoke of acres then and miles and masses,
Velocity and steam, cables that moored
Not ships but continents, world granaries,
The east-west cousinship, a nation's rise,
Hail of identity, a world expanding,
If not the universe: the feel of it
Was in the air – *"Union required the Line."*
The theme was current at the banquet tables,
And arguments profane and sacred rent
God-fearing families into partisans.
Pulpit, platform and floor were sounding-boards;

Cushions beneath the pounding fists assumed
The hues of western sunsets; nostrils sniffed
The prairie tang; the tongue rolled over texts:
Even St. Paul was being invoked to wring
The neck of Thomas in this war of faith
With unbelief. Was ever an adventure
Without its cost? Analogies were found
On every page of history or science.
A nation, like the world, could not stand still.
What was the use of records but to break them?
The tougher armour followed the new shell;
The newer shell the armour; lighthouse rockets
Sprinkled their stars over the wake of wrecks.
Were not the engineers at work to close
The lag between the pressures and the valves?
The same world then as now thirsting for power
To crack those records open, extra pounds
Upon the inches, extra miles per hour.
The mildewed static schedules which before
Had like asbestos been immune to wood
Now curled and blackened in the furnace coal.
This power lay in the custody of men
From down-and-outers needing roofs, whose hands
Were moulded by their fists, whose skins could feel
At home incorporate with dolomite,
To men who with the marshal instincts in them,
Deriving their authority from wallets,
Directed their battalions from the trestles.

THE GATHERING

*("Oats – a grain which in England is generally given to
horses, but in Scotland supports the people." – Dr. Samuel Johnson. "True, but where will you find such horses,
where such men?" – Lord Elibank's reply as recorded by
Sir Walter Scott.)*

Oatmeal was in their blood and in their names.
Thrift was the title of their catechism.
It governed all things but their mess of porridge

186

Which, when it struck the hydrochloric acid
With treacle and skim-milk, became a mash.
Entering the duodenum, it broke up
Into amino acids: then the liver
Took on its natural job as carpenter:
Foreheads grew into cliffs, jaws into juts.
The meal, so changed, engaged the follicles:
Eyebrows came out as gorse, the beards as thistles,
And the chest-hair the fell of Grampian rams.
It stretched and vulcanized the human span:
Nonagenarians worked and thrived upon it.
Out of such chemistry run through by genes,
The food released its fearsome racial products: —
The power to strike a bargain like a foe,
To win an argument upon a burr,
Invest the language with a Bannockburn,   3
Culloden or the warnings of Lochiel,   4
Weave loyalties and rivalries in tartans,
Present for the amazement of the world
Kilts and the civilized barbaric Fling,
And pipes which, when they acted on the mash,
Fermented lullabies to *Scots wha hae*.   5

Their names were like a battle-muster — Angus
(He of the Shops) and Fleming (of the Transit),
Hector (of the *Kicking Horse*), Dawson,
"Cromarty" Ross, and Beatty (Ulster Scot),
Bruce, Allan, Galt and Douglas, and the "twa" —
Stephen (Craigellachie) * and Smith (Strathcona) —
Who would one day climb from their Gaelic hide-outs,
Take off their plaids and wrap them round the mountains.
And then the everlasting tread of the Macs,
Vanguard, centre and rear, their roving eyes
On summits, rivers, contracts, beaver, ledgers:
Their ears cocked to the skirl of Sir John A.,
The general of the patronymic march.

* *"Stand Fast, Craigellachie,"* the war-cry of the Clan Grant,
named after a rock in the Spey Valley, and used as a cable message from Stephen in London to the Directors in Montreal.

(There follows an account of an insomniac dream by the then Prime Minister, Sir John A. Macdonald (1815–91), about the difficulties of a transcontinental railroad. He then plans how he can get the project through Parliament. After much difficulty and debate, the terms are finally ratified by the House and, as a consequence, British Columbia enters Confederation in July 1871.

Later, charges of corruption are made in the House against Macdonald's government. After a smashing attack by Edward Blake, leader of the opposition from 1879 to 1887, an election is called and Macdonald is defeated. Amidst party strife and divided councils about the routes of the proposed line, Alexander Mackenzie (1822–92) became Prime Minister in 1873.)

For forty years in towns and cities men
Had watched the Lines baptized with charters, seen
Them grow, marry and bring forth children.
Parades and powder had their uses then
For gala days; and bands announced arrivals,
Betrothals, weddings and again arrivals.
Champagne brimmed in the font as they were named
With titles drawn from the explorers' routes,
From Saints and Governors, from space and seas
And compass-points – Saints Andrew, Lawrence,
    Thomas,
Louis and John; Champlain, Simcoe; Grand Trunk,
Intercolonial, the Canadian Southern,
Dominion-Atlantic, the Great Western – names
That caught a continental note and tried
To answer it. Half-gambles though they were,
Directors built those Roads and heard them run
To the sweet silver jingle in their minds.

The airs had long been mastered like old songs
The feet could tap to in the galleries.
But would they tap to a new rhapsody,
A harder one to learn and left unfinished?
What ear could be assured of absolute pitch
To catch this kind of music in the West?

188

The far West? Men had used this flattering name
For East or but encroachment on the West.
And was not Lake Superior still the East,
A natural highway which ice-ages left,
An unappropriated legacy?
There was no discord in the piston-throbs
Along this Road. This was old music too.
That northern spine of rock, those western mountains,
Were barriers built of God and cursed of Blake.
Mild in his oaths, Mackenzie would avoid them.
He would let contracts for the south and west,
Push out from settlement to settlement.
This was economy, just plain horse-sense.
The Western Lines were there – American.
He would link up with them, could reach the Coast.
The Eagle and the Lion were good friends:
At least the two could meet on sovereign terms
Without a sign of fur and feathers flying.
As yet, but who could tell? So far, so good.
Spikes had been driven at the boundary line,
From Emerson across the Red to Selkirk,
And then to Thunder Bay – to Lake Superior;
Across the prairies in God's own good time,
His plodding, patient, planetary time.

Five years' delay: surveys without construction;
Short lines suspended, discord in the Party.
The West defrauded of its glittering peaks,
The public blood was stirring and protesting
At this continuous dusk upon the mountains.
The old conductor off the podium,
The orchestra disbanded at the time
The daring symphony was on the score,
The audience cupped their ears to catch a strain:
They heard a plaintive thinning oboe-A
That kept on thinning while slow feeble steps
Approached the stand. Was this the substitute
For what the auditorium once knew –
The maestro who with tread of stallion hoofs

Came forward shaking platforms and the rafters,
And followed up the concert pitch with sound
Of drums and trumpets and the organ blasts
That had the power to toll out apathy
And make snow peaks ring like Cathedral steeples?
Besides, accompanying those bars of music,
There was an image men had not forgotten,
The shaggy chieftain standing at his desk,
That last-ditch fight when he was overthrown,
That desperate five hours. At least they knew
His personal pockets were not lined with pelf,
Whatever loot the others grabbed. The words
British, the West instead of South, the Nation,
The all-Canadian route – these terms were singing
Fresher than ever while the grating tones
Under the stress of argument had faded
Within the shroud of their monotony.

*(Sir John returns to power in 1878 with a National Policy
of Protective Tariff and the Transcontinental.)*

Two years of tuning up: it needed that
To counterpoint Blake's eloquence or lift
Mackenzie's non-adventurous common sense
To the ignition of an enterprise.
The pace had to be slow at first, a tempo
Cautious, simple to follow. Sections strewn
Like amputated limbs along the route
Were sutured. This appealed to sanity.
No argument could work itself to sweat
Against a prudent case, for the terrain
Looked easy from the Lake to the Red River.
To stop with those suspensions was a waste
Of cash and time. But the huge task announced
Ten years before had now to start afresh –
The moulding of men's minds was harder far
Than moulding of the steel and prior to it.
It was the battle of ideas and words
And kindred images called by the same name,
Like brothers who with temperamental blood

Went to it with their fists. Canyons and cliffs
Were precipices down which men were hurled,
Or something to be bridged and sheared and scaled.
Likewise the Pass had its ambiguous meaning.
The leaders of the factions in the House
And through the country spelled the word the same:
The way they got their tongue around the word
Was different, for some could make it hiss
With sound of blizzards screaming over ramparts:
The Pass – the Yellowhead, the Kicking Horse –   7
Or jam it with *coureur-de-bois* romance,   8
Or join it to the empyrean. Eagles,
In flight banking their wings above a fish-stream,
Had guided the explorers to a route
And given the Pass the title of their wings.
The stories lured men's minds up to the mountains
And down along the sandbars of the rivers.
Rivalling the *"brown and barren"* on the maps,
Officially *"not fit for human life"*,
Were vivid yellows flashing in the news –
"Gold in the Cariboo," "Gold in the Fraser."
The swish of gravel in the placer-cradles
Would soon be followed by the spluttering fuses,
By thunder echoing thunder; for one month
After Blake's Ottawa roar would Onderdonk   9
Roar back from Yale by ripping canyon walls   10
To crash the tons by millions in the gorges.

The farther off, as by a paradox
Of magnets, was the golden lure the stronger:
Two thousand miles away, imagined peaks
Had the vacation pull of mountaineering,
But with the closer vision would the legs
Follow the mind? 'Twas Blake who raised the question
And answered it. Though with his natural eyes
Up to this time he had not sighted mountains,
He was an expert with the telescope.

*(Blake mounts another attack on Macdonald, but this
time it fails, in spite of his ringing declaration that it is*

impossible to build a road "over that sea of mountains".
Sir John goes to London to try to raise capital for the line,
but fails. He then looks nearer home for help and enlists
the aid of the canny western trader Donald Alexander
Smith (later 1st Baron Strathcona and Mount Royal) and
his cousin George Stephen (later Baron Mount Stephen).
With their many contacts and wide influence in the
western provinces they rally support and capital for the
line. In 1881, Parliament grants a charter to Stephen,
who becomes the first President of the Canadian Pacific
Railway. Stephen hires the American engineer William
Cornelius Van Horne, who arrives in Winnipeg in De-
cember 1881 to take charge of construction.)

Stephen had laid his raw hands on Van Horne,
Pulled him across the border, sent him up
To get the feel of northern temperatures.
He knew through Hill the story of his life   11
And found him made to order. Nothing less
Than geologic space his field of work,
He had in Illinois explored the creeks
And valleys, brooded on the rocks and quarries.
Using slate fragments, he became a draughtsman,
Bringing to life a landscape or a cloud,
Turning a tree into a beard, a cliff
Into a jaw, a creek into a mouth
With banks for lips. He loved to work on shadows.
Just now the man was forcing the boy's stature,
The while the youth tickled the man within.
Companioned by the shade of Agassiz,   12
He would come home, his pockets stuffed with fossils –
Crinoids and fish-teeth – and his tongue jabbering
Of the earth's crust before the birth of life,
Prophetic of the days when he would dig
Into Laurentian rock. The morse-key tick
And tape were things mesmeric – space and time
Had found a junction. Electricity
And rock, one novel to the coiling hand,
The other frozen in the lap of age,

Were playthings for the boy, work for the man.
As man he was the State's first operator;
As boy he played a trick upon his boss
Who, cramped with current, fired him on the instant;
As man at school, escaping Latin grammar,
He tore the fly-leaf from the text to draw
The contour of a hill; as boy he sketched
The principal, gave him flapdoodle ears,
Bristled his hair, turned eyebrows into quills,
His whiskers into flying buttresses,
His eye-tusks into rusted railroad spikes,
And made a truss between his nose and chin.
Expelled again, he went back to the keys,
To bush and rock and found companionship
With quarry-men, stokers and station-masters,
Switchmen and locomotive engineers.

Now he was transferred to Winnipeg.
Of all the places in an unknown land
Chosen by Stephen for Van Horne, this was
The pivot on which he could turn his mind.
Here he could clap the future on the shoulder
And order Fate about as his lieutenant,
For he would take no nonsense from a thing
Called Destiny – the stars had to be with him.
He spent the first night in soliloquy,
Like Sir John A. but with a difference.
Sir John wanted to sleep but couldn't do it:
Van Horne could sleep but never wanted to.
It was a waste of time, his bed a place
Only to think or dream with eyes awake.
Opening a jack-knife, he went to the window,
Scraped off the frost. Great treks ran through his mind,
East-west. Two centuries and a half gone by,
One trek had started from the Zuyder Zee
To the new Amsterdam. 'Twas smooth by now,
Too smooth. His line of grandsires and their cousins
Had built a city from Manhattan dirt.
Another trek to Illinois; it too

Was smooth, but this new one it was his job
To lead, then build a highway which men claimed
Could not be built. Statesmen and engineers
Had blown their faces blue with their denials:
The men who thought so were asylum cases
Whose monomanias harmless up to now
Had not swept into cells. His bearded chin
Pressed to the pane, his eyes roved through the west.
He saw the illusion at its worst – the frost,
The steel precision of the studded heavens,
Relentless mirror of a covered earth.
His breath froze on the scrape: he cut again
And glanced at the direction west-by-south.
That westward trek was the American,
Union-Pacific – easy so he thought,
Their forty million stacked against his four.
Lonely and desolate this. He stocked his mind
With items of his task: the simplest first,
Though hard enough, the Prairies, then the Shore
North of the Lake – a quantity half-guessed.
Mackenzie like a balky horse had shied
And stopped at this. Van Horne knew well the reason,
But it was vital for the all-land route.
He peered through at the South. Down there Jim Hill
Was whipping up his horses on a road
Already paved. The stations offered rest
With food and warmth, and their well-rounded names
Were tossed like apples to the public taste.

He made a mental note of his three items.
He underlined the Prairies, double-lined
The Shore and triple-lined *Beyond the Prairies*,
Began counting the Ranges – first the Rockies;
The Kicking Horse ran through them, this he knew;
The Selkirks? Not so sure. Some years before
Had Moberly and Perry tagged a route   13
Across the lariat loop of the Columbia.
Now Rogers was traversing it on foot,   14
Reading an aneroid and compass, chewing

194

Sea-biscuit and tobacco. Would the steel
Follow this trail? Van Horne looked farther west.
There was the Gold Range, there the Coastal Mountains.
He stopped, putting a period to the note,
As rivers troubled nocturnes in his ears.
His plans must not seep into introspection –
Call it a night, for morning was at hand,
And every hour of daylight was for work.

(Van Horne goes to Montreal to meet the Directors.)

He had agenda staggering enough
To bring the sweat even from Stephen's face.
As daring as his plans, so daring were
His promises. To build five hundred miles
Upon the prairies in one season: this
Was but a cushion for the jars ahead.
The Shore – he had to argue, stamp and fight
For this. The watercourses had been favoured,   15
The nation schooled to that economy.
He saw that Stephen, after wiping beads
From face and forehead, had put both his hands
Deep in his pockets – just a habit merely
Of fingering change – but still Van Horne went on
To clinch his case: the north shore could avoid
The over-border route – a national point
If ever there was one. He promised this
As soon as he was through with buffalo-grass.
And then the little matter of the Rockies:
This must be swallowed without argument,
As obvious as space, clear as a charter.
But why the change in Fleming's survey? Why   16
The Kicking Horse and not the Yellowhead?
The national point again. The Kicking Horse
Was shorter, closer to the boundary line;
No rival road would build between the two.
He did not dwell upon the other Passes.
He promised all with surety of schedule,
And with a self-imposed serenity
That dried the sweat upon the Board Room faces.

NUMBER ONE

Oak Lake to Calgary. Van Horne took off
His coat. The North must wait, for that would mean
His shirt as well. First and immediate
This prairie pledge – five hundred miles, and it
Was winter. Failure of this trial promise
Would mean – no, it must not be there for meaning.
An order from him carried no repeal:
It was as final as an execution.
A cable started rolling mills in Europe:
A tap of Morse sent hundreds to the bush,
Where axes swung on spruce and the saws sang,
Changing the timber into pyramids
Of poles and sleepers. Clicks, despatches, words,
Like lanterns in a night conductor's hands,
Signalled the wheels: a nod put Shaughnessy
In Montreal: supplies moved on the minute.
Thousands of men and mules and horses slipped
Into their togs and harness night and day.
The grass that fed the buffalo was turned over,
The black alluvial mould laid bare, the bed
Levelled and scraped. As individuals
The men lost their identity; as groups,
As gangs, they massed, divided, subdivided,
Like numerals only – sub-contractors, gangs
Of engineers, and shovel gangs for bridges,
Culverts, gangs of mechanics stringing wires,
Loading, unloading and reloading gangs,
Gangs for the fish-plates and the spiking gangs,
Putting a silver polish on the nails.
But neither men nor horses ganged like mules:
Wiser than both they learned to unionize.
Some instinct in their racial nether regions
Had taught them how to sniff the five-hour stretch
Down to the fine arithmetic of seconds.
They tired out their rivals and they knew it.
They'd stand for overwork, not overtime.
Faster than workmen could fling down their shovels,
They could unhinge their joints, unhitch their tendons;

196

Jumping the foreman's call, they brayed *"Unhook"*
With a defiant, corporate instancy.
The promise which looked first without redemption
Was being redeemed. From three to seven miles
A day the parallels were being laid,
Though Eastern throats were hoarse with the old
    question –
Where are the settlements? And whence the gift
Of tongues which could pronounce place-names that
    purred
Like cats in relaxation after kittens?
Was it a part of the same pledge to turn
A shack into a bank for notes renewed;
To call a site a city when men saw
Only a water-tank? This was an act
Of faith indeed – substance of things unseen –
Which would convert preachers to miracles,
Lure teachers into lean-to's for their classes.
And yet it happened that while labourers
Were swearing at their blisters in the evening
And straightening out their spinal kinks at dawn,
The tracks joined up Oak Lake to Calgary.

*("Number Two" is an account of the building of the line
along the precipitous North Shore of Lake Superior.
Pratt names this part of the land the "Laurentian lizard",
since its deep clefts and fissures were cut from the Laurentian Shield by the glaciers of the Ice Age. In spite of snow,
ice-storms, and floods, this section is finally well on the
way to being mastered.)*

NUMBER THREE

The big one was the mountains – seas indeed!
With crests whiter than foam: they poured like seas,
Fluting the green banks of the pines and spruces.
An eagle-flight above they hid themselves
In clouds. They carried space upon their ledges.
Could these be overridden frontally,
Or like typhoons outsmarted on the flanks?

And what were on the flanks? The troughs and canyons,
Passes more dangerous to the navigator
Than to Magellan when he tried to read
The barbarous language of his Strait by calling
For echoes from the rocky hieroglyphs
Playing their pranks of hide-and-seek in fog:
As stubborn too as the old North-West Passage,
More difficult, for ice-packs could break up;
And as for bergs, what polar architect
Could stretch his compass points to draught such peaks
As kept on rising there beyond the foothills?
And should the bastions of the Rockies yield
To this new human and unnatural foe,
Would not the Selkirks stand? This was a range
That looked like some strange dread outside a door
Which gave its name but would not show its features,
Leaving them to the mind to guess at. This
Meant tunnels – would there be no end to boring?
There must be some day. Fleming and his men
Had nosed their paths like hounds; but paths and trails,
Measured in every inch by chain and transit,
Looked easy and seductive on a chart.
The rivers out there did not flow: they tumbled.
The cataracts were fed by glaciers;
Eddies were thought as whirlpools in the Gorges,
And gradients had paws that tore up tracks.

Terror and beauty like twin signal flags
Flew on the peaks for men to keep their distance.
The two combined as in a storm at sea –
"Stay on the shore and take your fill of breathing,
But come not to the decks and climb the rigging."
The Ranges could put cramps in hands and feet
Merely by the suggestion of the venture.
They needed miles to render up their beauty,
As if the gods in high aesthetic moments,
Resenting the profanity of touch,
Chiselled this sculpture for the eye alone.

(Van Horne in momentary meditation at the Foothills.)

His name was now a legend. The North Shore,
Though not yet conquered, yet had proved that he
Could straighten crooked roads by pulling at them,
Shear down a hill and drain a bog or fill
A valley overnight. Fast as a bobcat,
He'd climb and run across the shakiest trestle
Or, with a locomotive short of coal,
He could supply the head of steam himself.
He breakfasted on bridges, lunched on ties;
Drinking from gallon pails, he dined on moose.
He could tire out the lumberjacks; beat hell
From workers but no more than from himself.
Only the devil or Paul Bunyan shared
With him the secret of perpetual motion,
And when he moved among his men they looked
For shoulder sprouts upon the Flying Dutchman.

But would his legend crack upon the mountains?
There must be no retreat: his bugles knew
Only one call – the summons to advance
Against two fortresses: the mind, the rock.
To prove the first defence was vulnerable,
To tap the treasury at home and then
Untie the purse-strings of the Londoners,
As hard to loosen as salt-water knots –
That job was Stephen's, Smith's, Tupper's, Mac-   18
    donald's.
He knew its weight: had heard, as well as they,
Blake pumping at his pulmonary bellows,
And if the speeches made the House shock-proof
Before they ended, they could still peal forth
From print more durable than spoken tones.
Blake had returned to the attack and given
Sir John the ague with another phrase
As round and as melodious as the first:
"The Country's wealth, its millions after millions
Squandered – LOST IN THE GORGES OF THE FRASER":
A beautiful but ruinous piece of music
That could only be drowned with drums and fifes.

Tupper, fighting with fists and nails and toes,
Had taken the word *scandal* which had cut
His master's ballots, and had turned the edge
With his word *slander*, but Blake's *sea*, how turn
That edge? Now this last devastating phrase!
But let Sir John and Stephen answer this
Their way. Van Horne must answer it in his.

INTERNECINE STRIFE

The men were fighting foes which had themselves
Waged elemental civil wars and still
Were hammering one another at this moment.
The peaks and ranges flung from ocean beds
Had wakened up one geologic morning
To find their scalps raked off, their lips punched in,
The colour of their skins charged with new dyes.
Some of them did not wake or but half-woke;
Prone or recumbent with the eerie shapes
Of creatures that would follow them. Weather
Had acted on their spines and frozen them
To stegosaurs or, taking longer cycles,
Divining human features, had blown back
Their hair and, pressing on their cheeks and temples,
Bestowed on them the gravity of mummies.
But there was life and power which belied
The tombs. Guerrilla evergreens were climbing
In military order: at the base
The *ponderosa* pine; the fir backed up
The spruce; and it the Stony Indian lodge-poles;
And these the white-barks; then, deciduous,
The outpost suicidal Lyell larches
Aiming at summits, digging scraggy roots
Around the boulders in the thinning soil,
Till they were stopped dead at the timber limit –
Rock *versus* forest with the rock prevailing.
Or with the summer warmth it was the ice,
In treaty with the rock to hold a line
As stubborn as a Balkan boundary,
That left its caves to score the Douglases,

And smother them with half a mile of dirt,
And making snow-sheds, covering the camps,
Futile as parasols in polar storms.
One enemy alone had battled rock
And triumphed: searching levels like lost broods,
Keen on their ocean scent, the rivers cut
The quartzite, licked the slate and softened it,
Till mud solidified was mud again,
And then, digesting it like earthworms, squirmed
Along the furrows with one steering urge –
To navigate the mountains in due time
Back to their home in worm-casts on the tides.

Into this scrimmage came the fighting men,
And all but rivers were their enemies.
Whether alive or dead the bush resisted:
Alive, it must be slain with axe and saw,
If dead, it was in tangle at their feet.
The ice could hit men as it hit the spruces.
Even the rivers had betraying tricks,
Watched like professed allies across a border.
They smiled from fertile plains and easy runs
Of valley gradients: their eyes got narrow,
Full of suspicion at the gorges where
They leaped and put the rickets in the trestles.
Though natively in conflict with the rock,
Both leagued against invasion. At Hell's Gate
A mountain laboured and brought forth a bull
Which, stranded in mid-stream, was fighting back
The river, and the fight turned on the men,
Demanding from this route their bread and steel.
And there below the Gate was the Black Canyon
With twenty-miles-an-hour burst of speed.

(ONDERDONK BUILDS THE "SKUZZY" TO FORCE
THE PASSAGE.)

'Twas more than navigation: only eagles
Might follow up this run; the spawning salmon
Gulled by the mill-race had returned to rot

Their upturned bellies in the canyon eddies.
Two engines at the stern, a forrard winch,
Steam-powered, failed to stem the cataract.
The last resource was shoulders, arms and hands.
Fifteen men at the capstan, creaking hawsers,
Two hundred Chinese tugging at shore ropes
To keep her bow-on from the broadside drift,
The *Skuzzy* under steam and muscle took
The shoals and rapids, and warped through the Gate,
Until she reached the navigable water –
The adventure was not sailing: it was climbing.

As hard a challenge were the precipices
Worn water-smooth and sheer a thousand feet.
Surveyors from the edges looked for footholds,
But, finding none, they tried marine manoeuvres.
Out of a hundred men they drafted sailors
Whose toes as supple as their fingers knew
The wash of reeling decks, whose knees were hardened
Through tying gaskets at the royal yards:
They lowered them with knotted ropes and drew them
Along the face until the lines were strung
Between the juts. Barefooted, dynamite
Strapped to their waists, the sappers followed, treading
The spider films and chipping holes for blasts,
Until the cliffs delivered up their features
Under the civil discipline of roads.

*(While Van Horne and his men fight the Rockies and the
treacherous, soft muskeg of the North Shore, Macdonald
battles his opposition in Parliament. At the same time
he has to drum up financial support in London and combat his own aging weariness. British Columbia, angered
at the delays in completion of the line, mutters about
secession and joining with the United States. With the
Canadian Union in peril, Macdonald girds himself for
one last battle, triumphs over his opposition, and finally
secures a loan from the London bank Baring Brothers.
The last gap in the mountains – between the Selkirks and
Savona's Ferry – is closed.)*

The Road itself was like a stream that men
Had coaxed and teased or bullied out of Nature.
As if watching for weak spots in her codes,
It sought for levels like the watercourses.
It sinuously took the bends, rejoiced
In plains and easy grades, found gaps, poured through
    them,
But hating steep descents avoided them.
Unlike the rivers which in full rebellion
Against the canyons' hydrophobic slaver
Went to the limit of their argument:
Unlike again, the stream of steel had found
A way to climb, became a mountaineer.
From the Alberta plains it reached the Summit,
And where it could not climb, it cut and curved,
Till from the Rockies to the Coastal Range
It had accomplished what the Rivers had,
Making a hundred clean Caesarian cuts,
And bringing to delivery in their time
Their smoky, lusty-screaming locomotives.

THE SPIKE

Silver or gold? Van Horne had rumbled *"Iron"*.
No flags or bands announced this ceremony,
No Morse in circulation through the world,
And though the vital words like Eagle Pass,
Craigellachie, were trembling in their belfries,
No hands were at the ropes. The air was taut
With silences as rigid as the spruces
Forming the background in November mist.
More casual than camera-wise, the men
Could have been properties upon a stage,
Except for road maps furrowing their faces.

Rogers, his both feet planted on a tie,
Stood motionless as ballast. In the rear,
Covering the scene with spirit-level eyes,
Predestination on his chin, was Fleming.
The only one groomed for the ritual

From smooth silk hat and well-cut square-rig beard
Down through his Caledonian longitude,
He was outstaturing others by a foot,
And upright as the mainmast of a brig.
Beside him, barely reaching to his waist,
A water-boy had wormed his way in front
To touch this last rail with his foot, his face
Upturned to see the cheek-bone crags of Rogers.
The other side of Fleming, hands in pockets,
Eyes leaden-lidded under square-crowned hat,
And puncheon-bellied under overcoat,
Unsmiling at the focused lens – Van Horne.
Whatever ecstasy played round that rail
Did not leap to his face. Five years had passed,
Less than five years – so well within the pledge.

The job was done. Was this the slouch of rest?
Not to the men he drove through walls of granite.
The embers from the past were in his soul,
Banked for the moment at the rail and smoking,
Just waiting for the future to be blown.

At last the spike and Donald with the hammer!
His hair like frozen moss from Labrador
Poked out under his hat, ran down his face
To merge with streaks of rust in a white cloud.
What made him fumble the first stroke? Not age:
The snow belied his middle sixties. Was
It lapse of caution or his sense of thrift,
That elemental stuff which through his life
Never pockmarked his daring but had made
The man the canniest trader of his time,
Who never missed a rat-count, never failed
To gauge the size and texture of a pelt?
Now here he was caught by the camera,
Back bent, head bowed, and staring at a sledge,
Outwitted by an idiotic nail.
Though from the crowd no laughter, yet the spike
With its slewed neck was grinning up at Smith.
Wrenched out, it was replaced. This time the hammer

Gave a first tap as with apology,
Another one, another, till the spike
Was safely stationed in the tie and then
The Scot, invoking his ancestral clan,
Using the hammer like a battle-axe,
His eyes bloodshot with memories of Flodden,   19
Descended on it, rammed it to its home.

*   *   *   *   *

The stroke released a trigger for a burst
Of sound that stretched the gamut of the air.
The shouts of engineers and dynamiters,
Of locomotive-workers and explorers,
Flanking the rails, were but a tuning-up
For a massed continental chorus. Led
By Moberly (of the Eagles and *this* Pass)
And Rogers (of *his own*), followed by Wilson,
And Ross (charged with the Rocky Mountain Section),
By Egan (general of the Western Lines),
Cambie and Marcus Smith, Harris of Boston,
The roar was deepened by the bass of Fleming,
And heightened by the laryngeal fifes
Of Dug McKenzie and John H. McTavish.
It ended when Van Horne spat out some phlegm
To ratify the tumult with *"Well Done"*
Tied in a knot of monosyllables.

Merely the tuning up! For on the morrow
The last blow on the spike would stir the mould
Under the drumming of the prairie wheels,
And make the whistles from the steam out-crow
The Fraser. Like a gavel it would close
Debate, making Macdonald's *"sea to sea"*
Pour through two oceanic megaphones –
Three thousand miles of *Hail* from port to port;
And somewhere in the middle of the line
Of steel, even the lizard heard the stroke.
The breed had triumphed after all. To drown
The traffic chorus, she must blend the sound

With those inaugural, narcotic notes
Of storm and thunder which would send her back
Deeper than ever in Laurentian sleep.

BIBLIOGRAPHY

I. PRIMARY MATERIAL

A. EDITIONS OF PRATT'S POEMS

Rachel: A Sea Story of Newfoundland in Verse. Pam. n.d. [privately printed, New York, 1917].

Newfoundland Verse. Decorations by Frederick H. Varley. Toronto: The Ryerson Press, 1923.

The Witches' Brew. Decorations by John Austin. London: Selwyn & Blount Ltd., 1925.

The Witches' Brew. Decorations by John Austin. Toronto: The Macmillan Company of Canada Ltd., 1926.

Titans ["The Cachalot", "The Great Feud"]. Toronto: The Macmillan Company of Canada Ltd., 1926.

The Iron Door [An Ode]. Decorations by Thoreau Mac-Donald. Limited to 900 copies. Toronto: The Macmillan Company of Canada Ltd., 1927.

The Roosevelt and the Antinoe. New York: The Macmillan Company Ltd., 1930.

Verses of the Sea, notes by the author, introd. by Charles G. D. Roberts. Toronto: The Macmillan Company of Canada Ltd., 1930.

Many Moods. Toronto: The Macmillan Company of Canada Ltd., 1932.

The Titanic. Toronto: The Macmillan Company of Canada Ltd., 1935.

The Fable of the Goats and Other Poems. Toronto: The Macmillan Company of Canada Ltd., 1937.

Brébeuf and His Brethren. Toronto: The Macmillan Company of Canada Ltd., 1940.

Brébeuf and His Brethren, 2nd and slightly revised ed. with new epilogue. Limited to 500 copies. Toronto: The Macmillan Company of Canada Ltd., 1940.

Dunkirk. Toronto: The Macmillan Company of Canada Ltd., 1941.

Brébeuf and His Brethren: The North American Martyrs. Detroit: The Basilian Press, 1942.

Still Life and Other Verse. Toronto: The Macmillan Company of Canada Ltd., 1943.

Collected Poems. Toronto: The Macmillan Company of Canada Ltd., 1944.

Collected Poems, introd. by W. R. Benét. New York: Alfred A. Knopf, 1945.

They Are Returning. Toronto: The Macmillan Company of Canada Ltd., 1945.

Behind the Log, foreword by the author. Drawings by Grant MacDonald. Toronto: The Macmillan Company of Canada Ltd., 1947.

Ten Selected Poems, with notes. Toronto: The Macmillan Company of Canada Ltd., 1947.

Towards the Last Spike. Toronto: The Macmillan Company of Canada Ltd., 1952.

Magic in Everything [Christmas card]. Toronto: The Macmillan Company of Canada Ltd., 1956.

The Collected Poems of E. J. Pratt, ed. with introd. by Northrop Frye, 2nd ed. Toronto: The Macmillan Company of Canada Ltd., 1958.

The Royal Visit: 1959. Toronto: C.B.C. Information Services, 1959.

Here the Tides Flow, introd., notes, and questions by D. G. Pitt. Toronto: The Macmillan Company of Canada Ltd., 1962.

B. PRATT'S NON-POETIC WORKS

Studies in Pauline Eschatology. Ph.D. Dissertation. Toronto: William Briggs, 1917.

"Canadian Poetry – Past and Present", *University of Toronto Quarterly*, VIII, no. 1 (Oct., 1938), 1–10.

C. WORKS EDITED BY PRATT

Heroic Tales in Verse, with Preface and notes. Toronto: The Macmillan Company of Canada Ltd., 1941.

Under the Greenwood Tree by Thomas Hardy. Toronto: The Macmillan Company of Canada Ltd., 1937.

D. CONTRIBUTIONS BY PRATT TO BOOKS

FOX, W. S., and JURY, WILFRED. *Saint Ignace: Canadian Altar of Martyrdom*, foreword by E. J. Pratt. Toronto: McClelland & Stewart Ltd., 1949.

II. SECONDARY MATERIAL

A. BOOKS OR SECTIONS OF BOOKS

BEATTIE, MUNRO. "E. J. Pratt", *Literary History of Canada*, ed. Carl Klinck et al. Toronto: The University of Toronto Press, 1965, 742–50.

BIRNEY, EARLE. "E. J. Pratt and his Critics", *Masks of Poetry*, ed. A. J. M. Smith, New Canadian Library. Toronto: McClelland & Stewart Ltd., 1962.

BROWN, E. K. *On Canadian Poetry*. Toronto: The Ryerson Press, 1943, 143–64.

COLLIN, W. E. *White Savannahs*. Toronto: The Macmillan Company of Canada Ltd., 1936, 119–44.

EDGAR, PELHAM. "The Poetry of E. J. Pratt", *Across My Path: A Literary Memoir*, ed. Northrop Frye. Toronto: The Ryerson Press, 1952, 109–17.

PACEY, DESMOND. *Ten Canadian Poets: A Group of Biographical and Critical Essays*. Toronto: The Ryerson Press, 1958, 165–93.

PARK, JULIAN (ed.). *The Culture of Contemporary Canada*. Ithaca: Cornell University Press, 1957, 54–5.

SUTHERLAND, JOHN. *The Poetry of E. J. Pratt: A New Interpretation*. Toronto: The Ryerson Press, 1956.

WELLS, HENRY W., and KLINCK, CARL F. *Edwin J. Pratt: The Man and his Poetry*, foreword by J. B. Brebner. Toronto: The Ryerson Press, 1947.

B. SPECIAL ISSUES

Canadian Literature, XIX (Winter, 1964), 6–32. "Salute to E. J. Pratt" [Fred Cogswell, "E. J. Pratt's Literary Reputation"; Paul West, "E. J. Pratt's Four-Ton Gulliver"; Vincent Sharman, "E. J. Pratt and Christianity"].

Douglas Library Notes [Queen's University, Kingston, Ontario], XII, No. 2 (Spring, 1963), "A Reminiscent Brew" [a note on the E. J. Pratt MSS. in the Douglas Library], 2; "The Lament of the Wets" [an early version of "The Witches' Brew"], 3.

Northern Review, V, 3 & 4 (Feb.–Mar.; April–May, 1952), E. J. Pratt, "The Great Feud", and John Sutherland, "E. J. Pratt: A Major Contemporary Poet", 36–64.

Tamarack Review, VI (Winter, 1958), 65–80. "A Garland for E. J. Pratt" [John Sutherland, "On His Seventy-fifth Birthday" [a poem], 65; A. J. M. Smith, "The Poet", 66–71; Murdo MacKinnon, "The Man and the Teacher", 71–4; Louis Dudek, "Poet of the Machine Age", 74–80].

C. DISSERTATIONS

BROTHER CONRAD, S. C. *The Dialectic of Love and Ferocity in the Shorter Poems of E. J. Pratt*. Manila, Philippines: Atenio de Manila University, 1964.

SISTER ST. DOROTHY MARIE, C.N.D. *The Poetic Imagery of Edwin John Pratt*. Ph.D. Dissertation, University of Ottawa, 1958.

D. SELECTED ARTICLES

BROCKINGTON, LEONARD W. " 'Tribute to a Poet': The Canada Council Medal to E. J. Pratt", *The Atlantic Advocate*, LII, No. 9 (May, 1962), 22–3.

DANIELLS, ROY. "Review of The Collected Poems of E. J. Pratt, 2nd ed.", *The Dalhousie Review*, XXXIX (Spring, 1959), 112.

DANIELLS, ROY. "The Special Quality", *Canadian Literature*, XXI (Summer, 1964), 10–12.

FRENCH, WILLIAM. "The Master Poet", *The Globe Magazine* (Published by The Globe and Mail Ltd., Toronto), Aug. 4, 1962, 8–11; Aug. 11, 1962, 15–17.

FRYE, NORTHROP. "Letters in Canada: Poetry", *University of Toronto Quarterly*, XXII (April, 1952), 269–75. Reprinted in Smith, *Masks of Poetry*, 97–103.

FRYE, NORTHROP. "The Personal Legend", *Canadian Literature*, XXI (Summer, 1964), 6–9.

FRYE, NORTHROP. "Silence Upon the Earth", *Canadian Poetry*, XXVII, No. 4 (Aug., 1964), 71–3.

FRYE, NORTHROP. "Edwin John Pratt, 1882–1964" [portrait], *Proceedings of the Royal Society of Canada* (4th Series, 1965), 161–5.

HORWOOD, HAROLD. "E. J. Pratt and William Blake: An Analysis", *The Dalhousie Review*, XXXIX (Summer, 1959), 197–207.

JOHNSTON, G. "Ned Pratt's Funeral", *Canadian Forum*, XLIV (June, 1964), 53.

KING, CARLYLE. "The Mind of E. J. Pratt", *Canadian Forum*, XXXVI (April, 1956), 9–10.

LIVESAY, D. "Polished Lens: Poetic Techniques of Pratt and Klein", *Canadian Literature*, XXV (Summer, 1965), 33–42.

MCGRATH, M. HELEN. "The Bard from Newfoundland: the Story of E. J. Pratt". *The Atlantic Advocate*, XLIX, No. 3 (Nov., 1958), 13–21.

O'BROIN, PADRAIG. "E. J. Pratt: 1883–1964", *Canadian Poetry*, XXVII, No. 4 (Aug., 1964), 63–4.

ROSS, MARY LOWREY. "Dr. E. J. Pratt: A Poet's Quarter-Century", *Saturday Night*, LXXIII, No. 3 (Feb. 1, 1958), 14–15, 35.

NOTES

(Some of the notes to *The Titanic*, *The Cachalot*, and *Brébeuf and His Brethren* are taken from Pratt's notes to his *Ten Selected Poems*.)

CARLO

1. *Second Peter, one, sixteen*: "For we have not followed cunningly devised fables, when we made known unto you the power and coming of our Lord Jesus Christ, but were eyewitnesses of his majesty."

THE IRON DOOR

1. *Plutonian*: Pluto was the Greek god of Hades, the place of the dead.
2. *Theban mockery*: Thebes' high walls were, according to Greek legend, moved into place by the lyre of the musician Amphion.

THE WAY OF CAPE RACE

1. *Cape Race*: easternmost point of land of Newfoundland, south of St. John's.
2. *Cabot*: John Cabot (d. 1498), Italian navigator and explorer, sailed for Henry VII of England. Discovered Newfoundland on June 24, 1497.

FROM STONE TO STEEL

1. *Java Man*: (Pithecanthropus) a genus of two species, *erectus* and *robustus*, regarded as primitive forms of extinct man known from skulls discovered in Java. Supposed to be one of the links between the apes and man. *Geneva*: headquarters of the League of Nations in the 1920s and 1930s. The League, without real power, fell apart early in the 1930s. The Geneva Convention is the international code of law pertaining to the conduct of nations in wartime.
2. *Aryan*: originally meaning a people sharing a common linguistic heritage. The term was perverted by the Nazis to mean the racial purity of the Teutons.

THE HIGHWAY

1. *Aldebaran*: a red star of the first magnitude, in the eye of Taurus; hence the Bull's Eye, *Alpha Tauri*. It is the brightest star in the Hyades.

THE DEPRESSION ENDS

1. *Prospero*: the ducal magician of Shakespeare's *The Tempest*.

2. *Tishbite*: 1 Kings xvii. 1-6. Elijah the Tishbite, of Gilead, was fed by the ravens when the rest of the Israelites were punished by God with drought and famine.
3. *Orion*: mighty Greek hunter. His name was given by the Greeks to one of the constellations. Much of the imagery that follows deals with similar mythical divinities and men whose names became attached to stars.
4. *Monoceros*: a constellation situated on the Milky Way, adjoining Orion and Canis Major, the Unicorn.
5. *Spica*: a star of the first magnitude in the constellation of Virgo, the Virgin.

THE STOICS
1. *Aurelius*: Marcus Aurelius (A.D. 121–180), Roman Emperor and philosopher. His *Meditations* is the profoundest work on the Stoic philosophy.
2. *panzers*: German armoured units in World War II.
3. *screaming comets*: probably refers to the dive-bombing Stukas used by the Germans in the same war.

COME AWAY, DEATH
1. *Piltdown scarps*: slope in Sussex where Piltdown Man, supposed to be an ape-like ancestor of modern man, was found. (Later discovered to be a hoax.)

THE TRUANT
1. *Lucretius*: Roman poet (94–55 B.C.). His poem *De rerum natura*, based on the philosophy of Epicurus, maintained that all nature, including the gods, was made of atoms.

THE CACHALOT
1. *da Gama*: Vasco da Gama (c. 1460–1524), Portuguese navigator, discoverer of the sea route to India.
2. *Cortez, Cavendish, Drake*: three great navigators of the sixteenth century.
3. *Van Tromp*: seventeenth-century Dutch admiral who defeated the English on several occasions.
4. *Taurian*: bull-like.
5. *North Saghalien*: Sakhalin, Russian island off the coast of Siberia.
6. *Cape Delgado*: on the east coast of Africa.
7. *kraken*: The term *kraken* strictly refers to a mythical sea-serpent alleged to have been seen by superstitious sailors off the coast of Norway, but is used also as a designation for the gigantic squid or devil-fish.

8. *Gorgonian*: The three Gorgons were mythical sisters who had serpents in the place of hair. Everyone who looked at Medusa, one of the sisters, was turned into stone.

9. *Nantucket*: New Bedford and Nantucket were the great whaling ports of New England.

10. *windjammer*: nautical slang, "taking the wind out of one's sails".

11. *looard beam*: Looard or leeward is that side of a ship opposite to that on which the wind blows; beam is the greatest width of a ship, that is, at the centre.

12. *Hard up*: to put the tiller quickly over to the windward side.

13. *gally*: to frighten, a word now practically confined to the vocabulary of New England whalers.

14. *drugg* (or drogue): a square piece of plank with a rope-tail spliced in its centre, and considered to hinder a whale's progress by at least as much as four boats. This is tied on the end of the line when it looks as if the whale is going to deplete the tub before he comes to the surface.

15. *piggin*: a small bucket.

16. *killers*: the *Orca gladiator*, a small whale with teeth in both jaws.

17. *breaches*: A whale is able to take an almost vertical leap completely out of the water, after the fashion of a salmon.

18. *hard-a-lee*: to put the tiller quickly over to the lee side.

19. *Bowhead*: a whale allied to the Greenland type, inhabiting Arctic and Antarctic waters.

20. *cutting stage*: a plank scaffolding suspended over the side of the vessel. The process of stripping the whale of its blubber is called "cutting-in".
    spade: sharp, square knife attached to a pole, and in shape like the blade of a paddle.

21. *trestle-cheek*: A trestle is a construction at the masthead to support the cross-trees and the topmast, and a cheek is a projection to support the trestle.

THE TITANIC

In the introduction to his notes on the poem in *Ten Selected Poems*, Pratt wrote:

The story of the *Titanic* is not primarily intended to be the record of a great disaster at sea. It is that indeed, for fifteen hundred persons were drowned when the big ship went down, but the loss of life as such would not account for the world-wide interest in the event, which is almost as keen today as it was thirty years ago. It is a study in irony, probably the greatest single illustration of the ironic in marine history. So completely involved was the ship in what we call the web of Fate, that it seemed as if the order of events had been definitely contrived against a human arrangement. Her sinking was absolutely incredible. She was described as the ocean lifeboat. There was never an event outside the realm of technical drama where so many factors combined to close all the gates of escape, as if some power with intelligence and resource had organized and directed a conspiracy. Apart from such provisions as constituted her normal protection like her immense size and flotation, her powerful engines and pumps – apart from all these, there were all around her within wireless touch eight ships, some of them like the *Olympic* and the *Baltic*, the biggest on the sea, talking to her, congratulating her on her maiden voyage as she sped along, and warning her of the presence of ice. The spectacle of the world's greatest ship slowly sinking to her doom in perfectly calm water, in weather ideally suited for the lowering of lifeboats, under a clear sky, sinking ablaze with electric light, sinking to the accompaniment of joyous music, was not only tragic but grotesque.

1. *The first lap*: The *Titanic* was launched a few months before her rival, the *Imperator*, which was being built by the Hamburg-American line. About a year elapsed between the launching of the *Titanic* and her trial trip, which might be considered as the second lap of the race, the third being the fatal voyage.

2. *her name*: This is the greatest source of irony in the poem. The Titans were gods who were defeated in battle by the Olympian Zeus. They were subsequently hurled down into a cavity below Tartarus.

3. *Geared to the rams*: The watertight doors in the bulkheads could be closed by a mechanism operated electrically from the bridge.

4. *double impact*: blow on bow and keel.

5. hubris: confident pride, so often punished in the Greek myths by divine retribution.

6. *Lloyd's*: the famous British institution of marine insurance and shipping intelligence.

7. *Godhaven*: a Danish settlement on the west coast of Greenland.

8. *clipper decades*: The fast square-rigged sailing ships in the nineteenth century could sometimes outsail the steamships.

9. *shags*: cormorants.
   mizzen peaks: the top of the aft-mast in a three-masted ship.

10. *Mother Carey eyes*: full of foreboding. Stormy petrels are sometimes called Mother Carey's chickens. The phrase is a sailor's adaptation of *mater cara,* an epithet of the Virgin Mary.

11. *Béchamel*: a rich white sauce named after Louis de Béchamel, steward of Louis XIV.

12. *Frank Gotch*: a famous wrestler, held world championship 1904, 1906–12; retired undefeated.

13. *Jeffries*: James J. Jeffries, world heavyweight champion, defeated in a famous fight at Reno, Nev., July 4, 1910, by Jack Johnson, first American Negro to hold world championship.

14. *growlers*: large boulders of ice almost submerged and very dangerous to navigation.

15. *The B.M.*: the British Museum, London.

16. *Bishop's Rock*: in the Scilly Isles on the approach to the English Channel.

17. *reciprocating*: The *Titanic* was equipped with both reciprocating and turbine engines.

18. *Starboard your helm*: Today the order would be "hard-a port" or "left rudder", as, subsequent to the time of the *Titanic,* the nautical directions have been changed to accord with the direction in which the wheel is turned. The orders given on the *Titanic* date back to the time when the ship was steered by a tiller, a post attached directly to the rudder, so that when the ship's head was to be turned to port, the tiller was put to the starboard side, which would turn the rudder to the left and the ship's head also.

19. *bilge turn*: the greatest point of curvature between the keel and the vertical part of the hull.

20. *Balkan scramble*: The captain's chief fear was that of panic in the steerage where hundreds from southeastern Europe, ignorant of English speech, might not understand the orders of the officers.

21. *Full noon and midnight*: As the boat lay level just before being lowered, the brilliancy of the lights from the portholes of the ship might be contrasted with the blackness of the sea observed from the starboard gunwale of the boat.

22. *gudgeon*: a metal eye or socket attached to the sternpost to receive the rudder pintle.

23. *beyond the red*: the danger-point of pressure on the gauge.

24. *hawse-holes*: the holes in the bows through which the cables or hawsers run.

25. *fiddley*: passage-way from a stokehold.
26. *Millet*: Francis (Frank) Davis Millet (1846–1912), fashionable American painter. His murals in the Custom-house, Baltimore, depicting the evolution of navigation, are generally considered to be his best work.
27. *Butt*: Major Archibald W. Butt (1865–1912), American army officer who was a personal aide to Theodore Roosevelt in 1908 and to President Taft from 1909 until his drowning.

BRÉBEUF AND HIS BRETHREN
1. *vows of rote*: Mechanical repetition had under the stimulus of the revival taken on an intense personal significance.
2. *St. Francis of Assisi* (1182–1226): left his father's home and devoted himself to a life of poverty and to the healing of the sick. The Franciscan order (named after him) modelled its practices upon the public life of Jesus.
3. *Vincent de Paul* (1580–1660): a French priest devoted to works of charity.
4. *Francis de Sales* (1567–1622): established the "congregation of nuns of the Order of the Visitation".
5. City of God: *De Civitate Dei*, the celebrated work of St. Augustine completed A.D. 426. Augustine was born in Numidia (Africa), in 354, went to Rome in 380, died in 430.
6. Imitatio: *The Imitation of Christ* by Thomas à Kempis (1380–1471).
7. *Theresa*: Saint Theresa (1515–82), reformer of the Carmelite Order. She is reputed to have had supernatural visions.
8. *John of the Cross*: a Spanish mystic (1542–91) who introduced reforms in the order of the Carmelites and was a poet of genius.
9. *Xavier*: St. Francis Xavier (1506–52), associated with Loyola in the founding of the Jesuit Society, 1534. He was known as "the Apostle to the Indies".
10. *Loyola*: Ignatius Loyola (1491–1556), a Basque soldier, after being wounded in the defence of Pampeluna (in Spain), went to the monastery of Montserrat and publicly renounced the profession of arms. His *Preludes* and *Spiritual Exercises* became the chief manual of instruction and inspiration for the Jesuits.
11. *Via Dolorosa*: the way of the Cross, the road leading to Golgotha over which Jesus passed on the way to the Crucifixion.
12. *Champlain*: Samuel de Champlain (1567–1635), founded

Quebec in 1608, was the first governor of New France, and explored the Huron Country, making it accessible to the missionaries and traders. It was under his direction that Brûlé visited the Huron districts in 1611.

13. *Le Caron* (compiler of the first Huron dictionary), *Sagard* and *Viel*: Franciscan missionaries. Viel was the first martyr to be killed by the Indians.

14. *sagamite*: corn-mush mixed with dried fish.

15. *Neutrals*: The main villages of the Hurons were situated in what is now Simcoe county, to the north of Toronto, the Algonquins being to the east and north, the Petuns (Tobacco Nation) to the southwest, and the Neutrals farther south in the general region north of Lake Erie.

16. *Arendiwans*: sorcerers.

17. *Richelieu*: Cardinal Richelieu (1585–1642), French statesman whose ambition to extend French power led him to the colonization of the New World.

18. *Kirke*: Sir David Kirke (1596–1656), who sailed up the St. Lawrence and captured Quebec in 1629.

19. *Aquinas*: St. Thomas Aquinas wrote the *Summa Theologica* between 1266 and 1273.

20. *Thirty Years*: the European Thirty Years War, 1618–48.

21. *Mazarin*: Jules Mazarin (1602–61), French chief minister who continued Richelieu's policies.
    Condé: Louis II de Bourbon (1621–86), Prince of Condé. Son of Henry II and military leader.

22. *Turenne*: Vicomte de Turenne (1611–86), French marshal, given command of French armies in Germany (1643). His victories laid the basis for French diplomatic triumphs in the Peace of Westphalia (1648).

23. Relations: *The Jesuit Relations*, accounts of missionary activities in the form of letters and reports to Superiors of the Order, on which this poem is largely based.

24. *Lady of Loretto*: Loreto, in Italy, is, according to legend, the place where the house of Mary, Joseph, and the child Jesus was taken by the angels after the power of the Christians was destroyed in Palestine in the thirteenth century.

25. *Blackrobes*: so called from the Jesuits' black cassocks.

26. *Martin, Baron*: French assistants. Abraham Martin came to Quebec with his wife and son in 1619 or 1620. The Plains of Abraham, outside of Quebec, are named after him.

27. *arquebus*: an old type of musket, fired from a rest.

28. Echon: The Huron name given to Brébeuf means "he who pulls the heavy load".

29. oki: spirit or demon.
30. *kibes*: blisters or ulcerated chilblains, especially on the heels.
31. *Medici confession*: a reference to the refined methods of extracting testimony under certain members of the Medici family, rulers of Florence in the fifteenth and sixteenth centuries.
32. *hatchet collar*: A form of torture was to place a ring of hot tomahawks around the neck of the victim.
33. *John of Patmos*: the writer of the Book of the Revelation who was exiled to the island of Patmos in the Mediterranean, where the Apocalypse was revealed to him.
34. aubade: a song or poem greeting the dawn, called also a matin song.
35. *"As naked as your hand"*: Lalemant's phrase.
36. *Fort Sainte Marie*: near what is now Midland, Ontario. The location of the site has been exactly determined and many of the original buildings are being reconstructed.
37. *Greater New France*: The mission to the Indians was seen by the political power as one of the means of colonization and consolidation.
38. *Dutch-armed*: Based on New Amsterdam (now New York), the Dutch were also contending for power in the New World and, like the English and French, sought allies among the Indian tribes.
39. *Fort Orange*: on the Hudson, now Albany, New York.
40. *Ossernenon*: now Auriesville, New York. There is a shrine here, Our Lady of the Martyrs, commemorating Isaac Jogues and other French missionaries killed by the Indians.
41. *the Iroquois Confederacy*: consisted of the Five Nations – Mohawks, Oneidas, Onondagas, Cayugas, and Senecas.
42. *The Passage*: the North-West Passage, the fabled route for ships from the Atlantic to the Pacific by way of North America.
43. *the Bourbons*: the dynasty of France established by Henry IV.
44. *Ragueneau's Relations*: written to his Superior Jerome Lalemant in Quebec, 1648–59.
45. *Calvados*: western shore of Normandy.
46. *Condé-sur-Vire*: a village on the river Vire in the southern part of Calvados and home of Brébeuf.
47. *Manresa*: a town in Spain near Montserrat, containing the church of Saint Ignacio built over the cave where Loyola lived and wrote.
48. *Loyola's mountains*: the heights of sacrificial devotion to the cause of Christ.

BEHIND THE LOG

1. *dead reckoning*: calculation of ship's position arrived at by laying out on the chart the course and distance covered by estimated speed through the water. Dead reckoning is used when the celestial bodies are obscured by cloud so that a "fix" cannot be taken with a sextant.

2. *Fisher*: John Fisher, First Sea Lord in the British Admiralty, responsible for the grand strategy of the Royal Navy during the First World War.

3. *Jellicoe*: Lord Jellicoe (1859–1935), Commander of the British Grand Fleet at the Battle of Jutland, 1916.

4. *at the Falklands cancelled Coronel*: In October 1914, at the Battle of Coronel, off South America, Admiral Graf von Spee's squadron defeated Admiral Sir Christopher Craddock's squadron. Fisher immediately despatched two battle cruisers to the area which met and destroyed von Spee's ships at the Battle of the Falkland Islands.

5. *kye*: slang name for thick cocoa traditionally made on Royal Naval vessels.

6. *W/T*: wireless telegraphy.

7. *para-a-vanes* (paravanes): depth control mechanism used to control cable in mine-sweeping operations.

8. *jag*: celebration (sl.).

9. *pennants 73*: Each ship was given a pennant number which was flashed at the beginning of a Morse code message directed to the ship by lamp.

10. *P.O.*: petty officer.

11. *asdic*: anti-submarine detection gear.

12. *Helmholtz and Doppler, etc.*: All these were mathematicians or scientists who contributed in some way to the theory or practice of the development of sound detection of submarines. Most notable among them are Hermann Helmholtz, German scientist, who worked on the nature of sound, among other things; Christian Doppler, German physicist, who discovered the Doppler effect, the change in tone of sound made by a moving object; and Paul Langevin, French physicist, who experimented with oscillators as a means of submarine detection during the First World War. Newton and Boyle were the seventeenth-century British natural philosophers whose experiments and theories laid the groundwork for modern physics.

13. *Willoughby, Chancelor, etc.*: explorers who searched for the fabled North-West Passage from the Atlantic to the Pacific.

14. *Green Four-O*: The asdic operator has found an echo

from a submarine forty degrees off the starboard bow.

15. *E.R.A.*: Engine Room Artificer.

16. *Harry one at the dip*: flag signal. Close up it meant: "I am the attacking ship and intend to attack with depth charge." At the dip, it meant: "Attack completed."

17. *Tirpitz*: Admiral Alfred von Tirpitz, the German officer chiefly responsible for the construction of the German fleet for the First World War, and whose aggressive strategies were in part responsible for the outbreak of the war.

18. *point-fives*: machine-guns of that calibre.

19. *four-point-sevens*: light quick-firing guns.

20. *the "patterns" and the "tubes"*: the pattern of depth-charge explosions versus the torpedo tubes.

21. *"in the rattle"*: accused of an offence under the Naval Discipline Act.

22. *Julianehaab*: fishing port on the south coast of Greenland.

TOWARDS THE LAST SPIKE

1. *St. Paul*: early Christian theologian (often quoted by Protestants).

2. *Thomas*: St. Thomas Aquinas (1226–74), theologian often quoted by Roman Catholics.

3. *Bannockburn* (1314), *Culloden* (1746): famous and bloody battles between the Scots and the English. The latter ended Bonnie Prince Charles Stuart's claim to the throne of Britain.

4. *Lochiel*: district of the Highlands that has many associations with the Jacobite rising of 1745.

5. *Scots wha hae wi' Wallace bled*: first line of patriotic Scottish song, closely associated with Bannockburn.

6. *the Lake to the Red River*: from Lake Superior to the Red River of the North. The Red River forms the boundary line between Minnesota and North Dakota, crosses the Canadian border, and continues north into the southern end of Lake Winnipeg.

7. *Yellowhead, Kicking Horse*: alternative passes through the Rockies. Yellowhead, elev. 3,711 feet, is west of Edmonton. The C.N.R. took this route. Kicking Horse, elev. 5,339 ft., is west of Calgary. The C.P.R. took this route.

8. coureur-de-bois: "woods-runner", the name given to the French or French and Indian half-breed trapper or hunter.

9. *Onderdonk*: Andrew Onderdonk, a contractor who hired Chinese coolie labour for the railroad.

10. *Yale*: a village east and slightly north of Vancouver, British Columbia, at the head of navigation on the Fraser River.

11. *Hill*: James Jerome Hill (1838–1916). Born near Rockwood, Ontario, Hill migrated to the United States and became a railroad promoter and financier. He eventually united his St. Paul and Pacific Railroad with the Canadian Pacific.

12. *Agassiz*: Louis Agassiz (1807–73), American naturalist and geologist.

13. *Moberly*: Walter Moberly (1832–1915), was assistant surveyor-general of British Columbia. In 1871 he was in charge of the Rocky Mountain and British Columbia surveys for the Canadian Pacific Railroad. He discovered Eagle Pass by observing the flight of eagles following a fish stream.
    Perry: Albert Perry, assistant to Moberly in a survey of 1866. Moberly maintained that Perry discovered Rogers Pass in this survey.

14. *Rogers*: Major A. B. Rogers. In 1881 Rogers explored the pass named after him through the Selkirk Mountains, north of Glacier Station, which was adopted by the C.P.R. for its main line. Snowslides and the difficulty of maintaining the road in winter led to the building of the Connaught Tunnel.

15. *watercourses*: Van Horne wished to build a complete land route following the shoreline of lakes (as was done). Public opinion was for a combination rail and ship crossing.

16. *Fleming*: Sir Sandford Fleming (1827–1915), first surveyor for the route of the railroad.

17. *Shaughnessy*: Thomas George, later Baron Shaughnessy (1853–1923), President of the C.P.R., 1898–1918. Joined the railroad in 1882 from the St. Paul Railway.

18. *Tupper*: Charles Tupper (1821–1915) was, from 1879 to 1884, Minister of Railways and Canals. He later became Prime Minister of Canada (1896).

19. *Flodden*: Battle of Flodden Field, 1513, in which the English defeated an invading Scots army under James IV.